MW00761555

ANTI-BLACK RACISM
AND
EPISTEMIC VIOLENCE
by
Dr. Kyra T. Shahid

Copyright © 2018 by Kyra Shahid

Sentia Publishing Company has the exclusive rights to reproduce this
work, to prepare derivative works from this work, to publicly distribute
this work, to publicly perform this work, and to publicly display this
work.

All rights reserved. No part of this publication may be reproduced,
stored in a retrieval system, or transmitted, in any form or by any
means, electronic, mechanical, photocopying, recording, or otherwise,
without the prior written permission of the copyright owner.

Printed in the United States of America
ISBN 978-0-9986948-1-8

Dedication

I dedicate this work to students like Amira Fruits, who find themselves searching for truth to speak to powers that attempt to hide it. Keep rising.

And to my most precious jewel Eden Fahari. May you also know the truth of who you are and use that truth to radically change the world.

Contents

Acknowledgements

This book is a reflection of my relationship with God and my ancestors. I am grateful to them for their prompting and guidance. I am also grateful to my family and friends who encouraged, prayed, and listened along the journey that has brought me to this point. I have an incredible village that walks with me. Thank you for being who you are in my life and in the lives of my beloved students. Your presence as parents, mentors, keynote speakers, dinner hosts, confidants, and role models for me, my daughter, and the students I have worked with at various universities help make it possible to envision what a better future looks like. I carry your wisdom in my spirit.

I am beyond grateful for the love and mentorship of my Sistah community: Christy, Dara, Porsha, and Morgan. The four of you have weaved the blanket that wraps me in healing, confidence, and courage. I honor you and the four incredible men alongside you. I am also grateful for my Sistah community within the Bryant Educational Leadership Group for your love and support as well as the energy you share to create places for our students to learn and embrace their purpose. I pray this work contributes to the nexus. This book contains pieces of my journey that began in my childhood and has been shaped by the balance of challenge and support I received at Central State University and Miami University. I appreciate every mentor, particularly Dr. Lovette Chinwah Adgebola and Dr. Denise Taliaferro Baszile, who have both influenced my ability to embrace my role in the classroom. I hope I make the kind of impact on students that you have made on me.

Teaching is not for the faint at heart and the transparency required to teach and write about a subject like this requires humility and bravery. I am grateful to Madame Phyllis Jeffers Coly for encouraging me to take up space and find the balance to write in wholeness. Thank you for your love and light. I had a vision for this book many years before I wrote it and I want to thank Audrey Calloway for capturing the photo that became the book cover. You were a burst of sunshine in my writing sky. Destiny Brown took that photo and recreated it with the elements of magic that say what could not be captured in the title. I thank you for your time and talent Destiny.

I would also like to say thank you to the five contributing student authors: Adrian Parker, Jr., Diamond Brown, Eseoghene Obrimah, Taylor Zachary, and Sequoia Patterson-Johnson. I am blessed beyond measure to work with students like you. You five are examples of why I do what I do. I hope this work catapults you towards your destinies. Additionally, I would like to thank my Xavier University community and the great people of Sentia Publishing for embracing my vision and helping to bring it to pass. I am also grateful to my smallest student, my daughter Eden Fahari. You have been willing to share your mother with so many students. You attend many of the events, class sessions, and conferences. You listen to my verbal processing and help me mold my ideas. We are a team and I am so blessed with the honor of being your mom. In closing, I want to thank every person who pauses to read this book. The labor that went into creating this book finds new meaning in the impact it has on your lived experiences. May peace be with you. -Kyra

Preface

When I began visualizing this book, I imagined that it would be a union between my voice and the voices of students. In my mind, this project could not legitimately demonstrate the necessity to create and validate knowledge production of students, particularly Black students, if that knowledge was not centered in the work. Therefore, I invited students to co-author portions of this book. Five students were able to meet and complete the challenge. Their wrestling, remembering, reclaiming, envisioning, and advising is the drum that gives this book its rhythm. The book begins with cover art created by Destiny Brown, a young aspiring artist and twin to one of the student authors. What Destiny created is an artistic version of a photo from my first trip to Senegal, West Africa. The image is filled with metaphor that embodies the underling messages in the book. As a descendant of enslaved Africans in America, my first *return* to Africa was quite sacred. There, I found pieces of me that I knew were missing but never thought I could recover. This book is a symbolic gesture to help others like me, recover pieces of self that are missing and broken, even if they are not as aware that they are lost.

In the image on this book cover, I am standing in front of the Atlantic Ocean. The water represents peace and reconciliation. I stand in the sand in front of the very body of water that served as a water grave for so many of my ancestors. My location symbolizes the divine power of Sankofa in the life of an African American. There is something to be said about the healing that takes place when one can recover from the past what it necessary to change the future. This kind of knowing, of (re)membering, creates a calm amidst chaos that nothing else in the Western world has for me. As I stood there in front of the ocean, I could feel the sand deepen beneath me, bringing me closer and closer to the earth. I thought about the heaviness of the challenges my students face and how the expansion of their knowledge had deepened their connection to self, to others, and to the divine. The outfit I wore that day was not planned, but standing there I felt my tie-dyed shirt blowing in the wind and I thought that I saw its blue and white pattern mirrored in the waves of the ocean. That moment symbolizes the middle passage within me, the cloak of history that I wear as a descendant of enslaved Africans. It also represents the healing wisdom and spiritual connection between the water and me. In the distance, you can see boats coming in, together. They are representations of the return of wholeness for all those whose lineage, customs, bodies, and hearts have been broken by the onslaught of anti-Black racism.

My raised fist represents our power. It is a nod to every person who has embodied resistance towards anti-Black racism. From my hand flies red, yellow, and green butterflies. It is a visual prayer for the transformation and release of the land, people, and resources that have been colonized, oppressed, and othered for so long. These butterflies represent new beginnings, reclamation of indigenous power, and the painful beauty of the diasporic migrations. They also symbolize the various cycles of growth and transformation that are necessary to escape and then rebuild an understanding of the subject matter within this book. There is no linear solution to anti-black racism or epistemic violence. However, the metamorphoses of self on an internal level and of systems on an external level initiate new phases of our existence. It is my hope that this book aids its readers in that process. I write in honor of my ancestors and with light for my students. My writing voice will alternate between speaking specifically to students and to all readers in an effort to hide that light in plain sight. My prayer is that this book serves as a conduit for people to touch God and be radically changed, empowered, and grounded in a full understanding of who you are and how your image of self impacts the world. May your reflections

bring healing, and may healing bring wholeness. Amen and

Ashe.

And they that shall be of thee shall build the old waste
places: thou shalt raise up the foundations of many
generations; and thou shalt be called, The repairer of the
breach, The restorer of paths to dwell in.
Isaiah 58:12

Introduction

I am an educator. I choose to work with college students because in them I see hope and despair, freedom and bondage, boldness and fear. They are complicated, sure, these young people with mixed and conflicting emotions and even more contradicting opportunities. I find meaning in helping them connect their sense of purpose with the careers they envision and service needed throughout the world. When I meet a new student, I tell them that the opportunity they have over the next four years is sacred because they will share space with people from all over the world that they may have never met otherwise. They will live amongst different cultures that they know nothing about. They will have the opportunity to explore who they are separate from their family (for the most part) for the first time in their lives. I think this is such an important moment of choice and exploration but I also recognize that many of them will have limited ideas about what to do with it.

I know that like me, they have spent years in school yet have not had much time to be creative, critical, or conscious. I also know that if they are Black, like me, they were having their mind assaulted no matter what schools they attended. Every semester, I look into the faces of Black students and I see familiar problems that they did not expect and were not prepared for. I watch them wrestle with how to deal with it. Some attempt to reinvent themselves as people who have escaped the issues altogether and are uninhibited by social constructions of race and racism, while others can't help but think about it or be reminded of it all the time. In the past five years, these college students have watched nightmares come alive all over the world and they have been reminded repeatedly that even paying tuition or wearing the school colors does not mean that they belong. They listened to the screams of

Trayvon Martin and saw no conviction for the man who murdered him. They lived in the cities where Michael Brown and Tamir Rice, and Freddie Gray, and Korryn Gaines, and Rekia Boyd, and Jordan Davis were all murdered. They were packing their things for college and leaving home when Sandra Bland died. They watched that video, and the one of Sam Dubose, and of Eric Garner, and of Philando Castile, and of Alton Sterling. They saw Black people gunned down in church because of racist bigotry and nightclubs sprayed with bullets because of homophobic and racist hate. They saw Black girls disappear and learned of Black people being sold into slavery at a time when most people around them were distracted by holiday shopping. This year alone, they saw news coverage of seventeen school shootings. They saw many of the shooters of innocent children handled and discussed in humane ways that had not been afforded to unarmed Black victims of gun violence. They questioned it. They picked up on subtle and not so subtle anti-Black justice, ant-Black politics, anti-Black media, and now they were experiencing a new level of anti-Black education. Prayers that they recited as children that included endings like, "if I should die before I wake," became everyday contemplations that began as "If I should die before I graduate..." I saw their puzzled faces after they spent hours in classrooms where none of this was mentioned. I felt their wrestling, as many of them did not come to college to fight social struggles; they came to get a degree. While some found comfort in the escape from reality that the classroom was generally providing, others buckled underneath the lack of harmony between the world around them and their world of study.

The problem is unflinching. For those who are undergraduates and are required to live on campus, they have their homes vandalized with "Nigger" written across their bulletin boards and nooses hung in their courtyards. They are bombarded with messages of anti-Black racism all the time. During the first week of class, well-meaning professors send them to writing and tutoring centers without knowing their academic abilities. Students form study groups around them and make it clear that they are not invited or expected to join. The toxic nature of their reality is even more complex, because contrary to the simplistic narratives told about these students, their lived identities are intersectional. The scarcity of resources to support them and deeply rooted nature of anti-Black racism makes any attention they draw to their reality seem like navel gazing and non-inclusive of the myriad of issues that others face around them. Many of them feel deeply betrayed, as they did not see nooses in the courtyards that were on the brochures of the university, yet they were learning more and more that their Black skin could get them into deadly trouble no matter how they behaved, what they studied, or what they believed. They were Black students, even if they were international, and that meant something. Anti- Black racism was breathing. Students who have had their cultures lumped under the identity of LatinX, found it difficult to talk about anti-Black racism, as the terms "Black and Brown" were often clumped together in ways that implied that their issues were exactly the same and made the discussion of anti-Black racism within *Brown* communities rare. This dichotomy was further complicated as news coverage of inhumane treatment of LatinX communities rose and the use of anti-blackness as a stepping stone for progression in LatinX communities resurfaced one more. Many white students and some Asian students had never had the space to talk about anti-Black racism openly and feared what their voice would sound like. Others saw no issues with anti-Black racism at all, and were growing increasingly tired with the seemingly illogical attention people were trying to bring to the matter.

As a student affairs practitioner, I attend conferences across the country and have met many individuals that work tirelessly to help these students succeed. We are the mentors, trainers, facilitators, advisors and negotiators of inclusion for the othered populations on predominately white campuses. I have studied the works of great theorists, educators, and social change agents who have worked to make higher education in the United States more diverse, inclusive, and equitable. Through divine connections, I have worked alongside allies of many different races and walks of life and we often circle back to the same question: How can we help? We see the four-year cycle of students who enroll, join organizations, and approach administration about seeking change on campus and we set our hearts to help them get as much justice as they can. What we know, and watch these students learn, is the historical memory within their organizations. We watch them learn that they are the latest model of a student who made similar if not the same demands ten years before them, ten years after their predecessor and so on. We connect them with like-minded students on other campuses, hoping our combined efforts will lead to significant and sustainable change. We remember the manifestos of demands and student protests that led to the creations of our own jobs, so we know the possibility of change. We find ourselves weighing the importance of empowering the institution against the importance of empowering our students because we know the two are not always aligned.

It is at this intersection of thought that this book was born. I write this book because I want to help students identify ways to situate their autobiographical narratives as intellectual activism while leveraging tools for their own healing. There is a great body of literature that will help give you the language to describe your experiences; however, I feel compelled to provide a new tool to help you navigate your experiences so that you might thrive and not just survive. The chapters in this book will shed light on what happens in academia that often damages the way you understand your reality. The words I use to describe this are **epistemic violence** (EV), actions that harm what knowledge is and how it can be created. Epistemic violence is the displacement or omission of certain knowledge in order to maintain power over others. It is the legacy of colonialism, of racism, of sexism. It is the lifeline to all of the phobic isms that vulgarize our differences and misrepresents them as deficiencies. Epistemic Violence is the pillar that makes Western and Eurocentric cultural thought and behavior appear superior to anything else. It is the academic muscle of white supremacy.

The subjects of anti-Black racism and epistemic violence are both timely and important because the relationship between the two is currently robbing millions of students of their educational experiences at primary, secondary, and post-secondary levels. When a class is labeled as "American History" but none of the scholarship in the syllabus includes writings by or about LatinX

Americans, African Americans, or Indigenous Peoples, epistemic violence occurs. When a student spends years excelling on standardized tests, but has no idea that there is running water and electricity in most African countries, epistemic violence occurs. When college courses that explicitly examine the histories and literature of non-western cultures are not core requirements for everyone, epistemic violence occurs. Epistemic Violence also happens when a place of learning espouses a mission of being a center for critical thinking and inclusion but continuously upholds policies, traditions, and standards that reinforce white supremacy, oppression, and dominance over the "other." These actions do not always appear "forceful," and are most often hidden in the lessons we do not remember learning; Lessons about what it means to be a woman, what it means to be White, to be Black, to be a "smart" or "intelligent."

There are systems at work every day that are attempting to take control of your narrative and tell you who you are or ought to be, both inside and outside of the classroom. The slightest distortion in your narrative not only changes how the world sees you, but it also changes your substance or worth. In a world of commodification and capitalism, the belief that knowing who you are makes who you are worth knowing has double meaning. When you are unaware of your own brilliance, it can be repackaged and sold to you. When you are not taught about the diversity of creativity that defines our world, your creativity can be standardized and stockpiled. When you are under the belief that your oppressors just don't understand that you have something to offer, you will spend your time proving your genius to a system that runs by siphoning it. My first question to you is one that was posed to me when I was a student: How do you fight in, for, and against a system all at the same time? I have contemplated this question for years as a student, as a professional, a woman, a mom, and a spiritually salient African American intellectual activist. All of these roles have led me to grappling with this question for one reason or another. The chapters in this book contain portions of my response to this question as well as the questions below. It is my hope that the thoughts expressed by me and the student authors will help you develop your own answers to these questions.

- How do professors and students move beyond building awareness to building intellectualism absent of Eurocentric control?

- How do we decolonize, rethink, and confront academic cultures that claim to be critically thinking and socially just, yet uphold standards, traditions, and epistemologies that maintain white supremacy and perpetuate anti-blackness?

- How can a classroom become a space of reconciliation and healing for students who are trying to dismantle anti-Black racism while living in an era where violence against Black bodies, Black minds, and Black futures is on the rise?

Part I: The Birth of Django Praxis

"Knowing how to be solitary is central to the art of loving.

When we can be alone, we can be with others without using

them as a means of escape."

— bell hooks

Chapter 1: An invitation

I met the incomparable Dr. James Cone in 2016 during his 'last lecture' tour at Xavier University. I told him about my research and the idea I had for this book. To my nervous delight, he was genuinely intrigued. I told him that anti-Black racism and epistemic violence were robbing our students of their education. He affirmed me and commented that it was also robbing them of themselves. He had written years ago in *Risk of Faith* that, "The power of definition is the key to one's ability to control one's future and thus one's perception of the self.[i]" He was not alone in his thinking. Audre Lorde wrote, "If I didn't define myself for myself, I would be crunched into other people's fantasies for me and eaten alive.[ii]" The power of self-definition was further affirmed when bell hooks used her writing voice to say, "If any female feels she needs

3

anything beyond herself to legitimate and validate her existence, she is already giving away her power to be self-defining, her agency[iii]." I told every student I have ever worked with, "Knowing who you are makes who you are worth knowing." Now, I was considering how the definition of self influences one's ability to create and dismantle anti-Black racism and epistemic violence.

Anti-Black Racism (ABR) is a socially-complex term that refers to the belief that all people assumed to be of African descent possess characteristics that distinguish them as inferior to another race, especially but not exclusively persons labeled as "White." This term also refers to acts of individual and systemic prejudice, discrimination, hatred, or apathy directed towards people labeled as "Black" based on pre-conceived notions, stereotypes, belief in Black inferiority, and/or fear of the "other." Anti-Black racism takes a toll on the definition of self. Now, when I say this in my classroom, students immediately think I am only referring to the "selves" in the room that are "Black." On the contrary, anti-Black racism takes a toll on every college student seeking a degree from an American college, and arguably every person in the world. The bondage that accompanies anti-Black racism creates a fixed place for the oppressors and the oppressed and all varying levels in between. Tell me this; who has more freedom, a man on the ground, or the man that is holding him to the ground? Who suffers more, the person being whipped, the person giving the beating, or the person who watches it happen? For some students, while growing up they heard their parents say, "this hurts me more than it hurts you," while they were being whipped for something they'd done wrong. Many have never reconciled such thinking and neither have their parents. There is no hope for reconciliation in such thoughts because measuring the degree of suffering that one person feels compared to another, who is in the same toxic relationship, only supports the myth that one of them can remain healthy. In our society it is often assumed that the presence of anti-Black racism creates self-depreciating attitudes and behaviors in Black people only, and that most non-Black people are unscathed, especially if they believe that they are not racist or anti-Black. However, the fixed relationship between the oppressor and the oppressed keeps us all "crushed into the fantasies" of colonialism and eats at our intelligence, our flesh, and our spirits. We all have our part to bear, or do we?

I challenge my students to develop their own responses to the question of whether or not anti-Black racism is *their* problem. In my classroom, I share a photo of a lynch mob that has captured, burned, and dismembered the body of a Black man. When I ask students to describe what they see in the picture, most focus on the lifeless body of the Black man hanging from the tree and become overwhelmed with grief for his family and for other Black people who had suffered from such heinous cruelty. I ask them how this incident influences or defines the person they are today. I then follow this question by asking them to tell me how they feel about the white people also pictured in the photo. I want to know how the smiling faces of those individuals influences or defines the person they are today. I share Dr. Degruy's lecture on Post-Traumatic Slave Syndrome and ask them to pay attention to the young white child that she mentions in a similar photo to the one I shared with them. Dr. Degruy points out that the young child is attending the "event" with her family and has had no say in the matter. She is being taught something that, while beyond her control, has grave impact on the woman she will become. The child did not ask for or generate the

An Invitation

anti-Black racism she was being taught, but it's presence in
her life as the way of thinking and knowing what's what in
the world (epistemology) was the only lens she had been
given. Historical evidence on what has been taught in
American classrooms make it safe for us to assume that this
child would rarely come into contact with any literature,
psychological treatment, or educational experiences that
would disrupt her foundation. The idea that Black people
were inferior and thus deserving of acts of discrimination
and hatred seemed as harmless and normal to her as
stepping on ants when she walked. Whether she embraced
or loathed such thinking would do little to disrupt the rapid
disregard every level of schooling would have to the
presence of the theory of justified belief she learned that
day. Dr. Degruy then comments that the girl in the photo is
now the age of the grandparents of the students in my
classroom.

An Invitation

Most college students today have not been asked to consider the psychological impact that anti-Black aversion has on the definition that they have of their selves. This is especially true and concerning for white people. Since racism is about othering, it is often easier to discuss it in terms of how one interacts with their other. Thus most who have participated in dialogues on racism have spent much of that conversation exploring how they have treated their other and/or how their other has treated them. I'd like to challenge you to reflect on how anti-Black racism impacts you. This question is not about whether or not you have ever committed a racist act or had a racist thought. It goes deeper than the surface manifestations of anti-Black or racist behaviors. Are you aware of the ways that anti-Black racism has influenced what you think about yourself? Does your definition of who you are make you more or less inclined to believe that you are personally connected to anti-Black racism? Why or why not? What, in your mind, is true about anti-Black racism and how do you know that it is "truth"?

When students respond to these prompts, they are often "shook" by what they learn about themselves. While these statements are not all-encompassing of all students or all racial identities, they are reoccurring sentiments I hear from students year after year. Black young women admit that they are ashamed that they are thinking anti-Black thoughts about other Black girls. White young men are deeply troubled and ashamed that they hate to look at their own reflection and are terrified to ask certain questions of their grandparents because they are unsure of what they will learn about their family. Latina women lower their heads, recalling what their mothers have told them about Black men and remembering the differences in the treatment of them and the darker-skinned cousins.

An Invitation

Multiracial students write about feeling torn and often unwilling to embrace the "white" portion of their identity because they are ashamed of what whiteness means, while others wrestle with embracing the "Black" portion of their identity because Black in their minds means lazy. They are startled when they hear their Black peers say things like, "I never thought of myself as being Black because my parents told me that too. It wasn't until college that I started redefining Black for myself."

When James Cone wrote that "the power of definition is the key to one's ability to control one's future and thus one's perception of the self,[iv]" I like to think he was saying that what we think about ourselves regulates the significance of any change in our future. Addressing anti-Black racism therefore is not just about changing the way the world sees Black people, but about discerning how the world's perception of Black people impacts how all people

An Invitation

define self. James Baldwin once remarked that even a white person experiencing the greatest of suffering in America will find solace in the thought that at least, they are not Black. The definition of self, even the subconscious self, is an indicator of how profound the wound of anti-Black racism and epistemic violence is. This look inward is a game changer. It is where students should first begin dismantling anti-Black racism.

Knowing who you are and owning your ability to define yourself is not an expectation or right practiced consistently in our society. Throughout history, various leaders have questioned the identity of this country based on its inconsistent and often contradicting definition of self. Dr. Martin L. King, Jr., a pillar of racial justice, compelled this country to think about its identity crisis by demanding that America know and acknowledge herself based upon the creeds of our founding documents and declarations that named her as a land of freedom, liberty, and justice for all. Students in the 1960s also demonstrated the power of a reality check by asking institutions to take a look in their figurative mirrors and demanding that colonists who oppose immigration engage in some reflective soul searching. Some of these students were first year college students who organized sit-ins at lunch counters and kept composure in the face of ruthless hatred, partly because they were unyielding in their self-awareness and unwilling to compromise their character because its validation was a root in their cause. But what is it about our society that keeps us cycling back to the same soul searching decade after decade in regards to anti-Black racism? Many students genuinely want to know how it is possible that the demands they are making of their institutions today are identical to demands that were expressed by college students 50 years ago. They recognized then, as they do now, that the institution offered a response and put some action into play towards addressing the matter. So how does the problem resurface, or never go away?

It is a question that sheds light on the dearth of action that is inherent in a system that often uses words like awareness and care as proverbial buffers against systemic change. The question is further complicated if you embrace the possibility that knowing who you are and doing the laborious work of cleansing your perception is convoluted when the lens you have or tools you have are not your own. What happens to children who grew up in the 1960s and learned that Africa had no history (except as the birthplace of slaves) and the most viable tools for building civilization and democracy were European? What happens when that child becomes an adult and gains access to a contrasting truth but knows that truth has little to no currency in the system they live in? How do they grow their children?

An Invitation

What truth do they hold to be self-evident? What happens to their child, who goes to school thinking that they are both smart and adorable, but then spends the next twelve years learning that people who look like them are inferior, and that any knowledge produced by non-European/non-Western entities is both secondary and less valuable (if valuable at all)? *Epistemic violence happens*, therefore making it all the more difficult for that child to ever truly know their selves. Earlier in the introduction of this book, I provided a definition and examples of epistemic violence (EV). I described epistemic violence as intentional uses of power that cause harm towards the way one can understand their reality. It includes actions that serve to insure that your understanding of what knowledge is and what is considered "knowledge" is maldeveloped so that power over oppressed communities can stay in place. Epistemic Violence refers to the forceful displacement of knowledge and ways of knowing in order to maintain dominance over oppressed communities. Gayatri Chakravorty Spivak (1988) first used this term to identify a number of projects in history, philosophy, and literature that indorsed claims to knowledge that identified colonized communities as "other." These actions helped individuals define themselves as being the creators of certain knowledge that had been stolen or distorted from colonized communities.

These actions also created a hierarchy of knowledge that helped mostly white individuals determine that their ability to know and to produce knowledge was more advanced or superior to the ability of others, particularly along the lines of literacy and language. Thomas Teo (2008) expanded on Spivak's use of epistemic violence and argued that it was a dangerous method of manufacturing theory and interpretation that creates negative consequences for the "other." According to Teo (2008), this negative impact includes "misrepresentations and distortions …neglect of the voices of the 'other'… statements of inferiority, and … recommendations of adverse practices or infringements concerning the 'other'" (p.58)[v]. My mentor and dissertation advisor, Dr. Denise Taliaferro Baszile (2006)[vi] adapted the term epistemic violence to describe activities in the academy in which one professes a commitment to critical thinking and social justice but continues to prescribe to standards, traditions, and ways of knowing that maintain hegemony.

On the average college campus today, students are experiencing these various levels of epistemic violence continuously and unknowingly. Therefore, when I ask them to engage in this kind of soul searching, they are unaware that their soul has been lost. Malidoma Patrice Somé[vii] proposes that when an individual has another culture's knowledge within them in place of their own, it makes that culture's spirit live in them. This kind of soul displacement, if you will, was described in the letters of Willie Lynch. When someone can control the way you think or what you have access to think about, they can control you and use you as a conduit of their agenda without your permission or awareness or intentionality. Therefore, you do not have to be "racist," the knowledge you use to understand the world will do that for you. The legacy of isolation and colonialization that lives on through Western and Eurocentric epistemologies can thus isolate one from their soul (the seat of your will, intellect, and emotions) and continuously distort your reality. As Americans, we will firmly believe we are wholesome and committed to the greater good, because our knowledgebase heavily prevents us from being able to validate worldviews that could teach us otherwise. As institutions, we will hold firmly to broken and passive pedagogies and practices while seeing ourselves as spaces of critical thinking and social justice, because the system we use to credentialize and legitimize knowledge offers narrow pathways for new knowledge to emerge. Change seeps in slowly, and the discomfort one feels when the foundation of what they know is disrupted, keeps us fearfully grounded in trusting a path that does not belong to us.

This is especially true and concerning for Black students, as the combination of anti-Black racism and epistemic violence almost guarantees that they will seldom access and explore their thinking through lenses that are their own or free from Eurocentric gaze and control. While culturally responsive teaching is being embraced on a larger scale and strides have been made to make the academic classroom more inclusive, such practices are the exception and not the norm. Is there no hope for a fully inclusive, Black-embracing, epistemically healthy

An Invitation

American university? Should students pack their bags now and walk away from completing their college education? What more can be done?

In the introduction of this book, I describe attending college as an important moment of choice and exploration. Students will live amongst different cultures that they know nothing about, and may not learn about in their classroom as much as they will on the yard. They will have the opportunity to explore their identities in new ways. Therefore, the realization that epistemic violence has been present in their life can give them a starting point from which to begin that exploration. I often hear students say that the only thing they can do to overcome anti-Black racism is to build awareness, acknowledge their privilege, and work to create space for the marginalized voices among them. I see them volunteer tirelessly, serve in countries that are in need, and participate in various organizations that allow them to address a social ill. The desire in the hearts of college students to make a positive impact in this world is breath-giving. I ground my own sense of purpose in helping them to make better connections to who they are and how they can impact the world through their vocation. However, what they want to know and what I hope you can gain from this chapter, are tools to help you and others not merely sustain in the world we live in, but radically change it. What I am talking about is fighting in, for, and against a system simultaneously. It is a tri-fold approach that requires creativity, redemption, and reclamation. So much of who you are is intricately woven into the fabric of the society in which you live. Ever heard the saying, a trifold cord is not easily broken? You will need some intellectual weaponry and spiritual dexterity to achieve the kind of wholeness that starves the seeds of anti-

Black racism that are nourished by systems of epistemic violence.

I am sure by now someone has told you that education is important. If not, grab your highlighter because here it comes: Education is important. It is a gateway to success and attending college is an indispensable and useful component to your journey towards self-actualization. If you are an African American student, education has served as a way out of oppression for your ancestors who were forced to learn and adopt the ways of the West. Malcolm X said that "Education is the first step towards solving any problem that exists anywhere on this Earth which involves people who are oppressed[viii]." What is the second step? Michelle Obama said, "You have to stay in school. You have to. You have to go to college. You have to get your degree. Because the one thing people can't take away from you is your education. And it is worth the investment." What makes it *your* education?

Schooling only becomes education when the student takes an active and conscious role in discerning and acquiring the knowledge they consume and create. Without such intentions, education remains under the auspices of schooling and someone or something else controls and reserves ownership over what you know. It's not your education simply because you pay for it or because you complete what is required of you. One must keep in mind that spaces that are oppressive will not intentionally aid you in achieving liberation. Nevertheless, the tools you need are mostly hiding in plain sight right among you because it is expected that you will be well "schooled" in looking past them. Additionally, the nature of today's collegiate experience embraces inundation and over-extension as commonplace. Many students are not in control of their schedules and exert excessive amounts of energy trying to keep up, never getting ahead. Therefore, the idea that you would read books or complete projects that are not on your syllabus or required in any way, reads as punishment or just simply unrealistic. So, you trust that people who have very limited knowledge of who you are or what you intend to do in this world, will fill your intellectual gaps for you. You invest hundreds of hours acquiring knowledge but you know little of its origins and have limited resources for comparison and even less time for discerning what your mind makes of the information. You are expected to be consumers of knowledge more than you are expected to be producers of it. Finding a way "out" through education, however, will require active and intentional creativity in defining who you are and what you know.

And so, this chapter is an open invitation to begin exploring who you are in relationship to the terms anti-

An Invitation

Black racism and epistemic violence. You can begin this process by constructing a racial autobiography. Take a journal and explore your first memories of race and racism. Ask yourself who you are and what role race plays in your life. How has anti-black racism impacted your education and your relationships with others? How has it impacted the way you see yourself? If given the choice, could being a different race give you more or less freedom to be who you believe yourself to be? Why or why not? Make a list of the ways you have learned about anti-Black racism. What is missing from your list and why? Once your reflection is complete and you are more consciously aware of yourself in terms of anti-Black racism and epistemic violence, I want you to begin exploring what it would take to move you beyond awareness to conscious action. Some of you may be hyper aware of the role race plays in your life and beyond frustrated with the mass deception that prevents social healing. How do you heal anyway? Some of you may be exploring these questions for the first time and feel overwhelmed by the onslaught of questioning. How do you repair the gap in consciousness that has existed for so long?

I believe there is a figurative bridge that provides passage from awareness to action. This bridge is not always in plain sight, as dominating ideologies perpetuate fog that obscures our views. However, we are not passive objects of historical or contemporary trauma. We are not tabula rasa (blank slate). If we are diligent in remembering that there is a bridge and that there is more work to do than simply clearing the fog that obscures the bridge, we can walk into new ways of being. As human beings, our limitations rest only in our ignorance. Do not count yourself out because you are young, or female, or whatever you may be told places a limit on how far you can go. You are the Sun. Your energy stimulates growth all around you but if you

An Invitation

stay in one place too long you could cause harm. So you must evolve. Resist. Re-exist. Move forward. Search within and expose yourself to the fullness of what's there. There you will find and redefine your truth. You will also discover that such work is not necessarily a move forward but perhaps a course correction so that forward becomes a possibility. You will also discover that you can turn your critical self-reflection into public intellectual activist work. The challenge herein is to regain and retain personal power and strong self-identification absent of anti-Black standards. This work begins with critically conscious reflection that orients the self in ways that permit us to be in relationship with others without using them as a means to escape pain, emptiness, guilt, or trauma. Such work is the foundational building block to addressing anti-Black racism and epistemic violence. It is my hope that you accept and complete the challenge.

An Invitation

Chapter 2: A Bridge Called Your Mind

Students sat on every available surface in my office. There were two students in chairs, one lying on their belly across the floor and three others sitting on the floor, with their legs protruding from the opening of the door into the common area of the office. It was not a sit-in or protest, nor was there a major crisis; it was an impromptu cypher and for my students that means comfort. We were generating *Django praxis*. Django is a term that means "I awake." It means to take a situation that seemed doomed to fail, and turn it into an overwhelming success. Django praxis is the process of enacting and embodying lessons and skills learned from situations that were intended for your demise. Django praxis is about resurrecting, recovering, redirecting, and realizing who you truly are. That day, on the floor of my office, students were discussing ways to situate their

29

autobiographical knowledge as intellectual activism, even though that's not how they would describe it. They were not consciously aware that they had engaged in Django praxis in our classroom and had been participating in their own healing through music, media, poetry, and drama. Yet, their subconscious vibes generated a sequence as eloquent as Duke Ellington and John Coltrane's synchrony in *In a Sentimental Mood*. They were repairing the breach for and with one another.

I remember this day because the energy in the room felt magical. I could tell they felt free. It was not an enchanted feeling like we were in a wonderland, but a child-like freedom that a kid experiences when they realize their parents are not watching and they can play as wild and free as they want. When I was a child, these moments were times when my imagination soared and my dance moves were perfected. I knew I did not have to explain myself and

A Bridge Called Your Mind

I could make sense of whatever I wanted to. I was not concerned about protecting myself (as most children aren't), so I tested the limits of my strength mentally and physically as I engaged the world around me. College students rarely experience this freedom and often turn to unhealthy practices as a means of escape. Others have forgotten such freedom, as they are constantly entangled by barriers disguised as policies, rules, and measurements that control the flow of imaginative power they can use. For many students that I know, their current lives keep them too contorted for them to have time to explore their imagination, as they are preoccupied by trying to appear as non-stereotypical or non-threatening. Unaware of just how deeply the compromise distorts their reality, they often contort further trying to reshape some sort of justice. Django praxis thus becomes realignment. It is a release of the pressure valve that dominating cultures use to control the flow of information and creativity that one can experience.

I have adopted the term Django praxis to describe the use of critically conscious autobiography as public intellectual activism. I wholeheartedly believe that the intellectual and spiritual death of young minds is perhaps one of the greatest atrocities of epistemic violence. Therefore, I have dedicated my research agenda to preventing epistemicide. I began this process in graduate school. It was there that I became acutely aware of the many traditions that deem certain ways of strategizing, theorizing, investigating, and understanding knowledge as non-applicable to serious academic work. My interest in student affairs and curriculum theory also exposed me to the various customs of academic commodification that often prohibit discursive knowledge from being credentialed. Among these were most practices both inside and outside of the classroom that sought to address or dismantle racism. Another gap was in the use of spiritual approaches outside of the confines of academic departments or student centers deemed to be appropriate places for such work. This created quite the conundrum for me, because I knew that a sense of spirituality was a decreed lifeline of the African American community and the epicenter for transformative resistance. My unwillingness to compromise this knowledge led me to researching the root causes of its absence and/or lack of acknowledgement in academe. I first explored the concept of epistemic violence in my dissertation and used spirituality as a tool to combat the anti-Black racism I discovered at its root. My dissertation gave way to the creation of the course, for which the book is published, and this book provides the platform for a contingency of students to engage in Django praxis; a concept birthed out of a process of bridging the gap between spirituality, intellectualism, and leadership on college campuses.

History suggests that spirituality has played a vital role in the emergence, persistence, and existence of counter-narratives to the normalcy of anti-Black racism and epistemic violence on college campuses. For most, spirituality requires a sense of faith to dare your mind to go beyond what your eyes can see, or what your mind can rationalize. Faith is a requirement for Django praxis and thus necessary to combat anti-Black racism and epistemic violence. It is important to note here that I came to my understanding of faith and spirituality through African American Christian Spirituality and Black liberation theology. When examining a construct as vast as spirituality, it is imperative to be clear about how I use the term. Accordingly, spirituality is defined as a personal commitment and belief in an interconnecting power that allows one to gain an understanding of a purpose greater than one's self and of an obligation to live by and express respect, love and interdependency of all. The nature of spirit and spirituality has different meaning and value in western and non-western cultures that are too vast to diligently discuss here. However, I will say here that the notion of spirituality that I utilize entails activity that connects and ties people together, be it intellectually or otherwise. It is nonconsequential of any religious belief and serves as a positive approach to transformative practices. My notion of spirituality is about tapping into energies that cultivate resistance to oppression and generate healing, restoration, and creativity.

When I reflect back on that day in my office with students, I am reminded of how important my notion of spirituality has been to the existence, preservation, and sometimes resurrection, of epistemologies that challenge anti-black racism. We began our reflection journey in this book by examining self and exploring how critical self-awareness can help us move towards action. The second challenge I want to engage centers on the question: How do we decolonize, rethink, and confront academic cultures that claim to be critically thinking and socially just, yet uphold standards, traditions, and epistemologies that maintain white supremacy and perpetuate anti-blackness? It is a loaded question and a simple response could be Django praxis. However the fullness of the response is not a rational concept and cannot be reduced to neat conceptual categories with step by step instructions. Remember, there is no linear or singular response to anti-Black racism and epistemic violence. Nevertheless, I have put language to some discursive practices that can help you deepen your capacity to decolonize, rethink, and confront anti-Black racism and epistemic violence.

A Bridge Called Your Mind

To do this, I want you imagine a window with four panes. Each pane contains a different form of glass: Bulletproof glass; two-way mirrored glass; tinted glass; and stained glass. Together the four panes create a tool for developing and maintaining a viewpoint that is resistant to standards, traditions, and epistemologies that maintain white supremacy and perpetuate anti-blackness. I first introduced this concept of a four-pane window in, "The Power of Revolutionary Thought: Waging Curriculum Warfare on the Racial Injustices in Academia.[ix]" I developed the window as a means to show Black intellectuals how they could successfully establish and sustain healthy ways of knowing. The chapter was a review and adaptation of the work of Sidney Walton, an educator and curriculum theorist from the 1960s and member of The Black Panther Party. What I learned from his work and from the windowpane I constructed was the vitality of such a tool for people who live the metaphysical dilemma of being Black and conscious on a daily basis and their allies.

In this window, the first pane of bulletproof glass is for protection from systemic weapons of intellectual destruction. This pane is essential, as it is the main source of protection against epistemic violence. The exclusion of certain knowledge in textbooks, omission of the denial of aspects of history, and quiet exemptions of any wrongdoing in this process are traditional forms of epistemic violence. Indeed no one is held accountable for the cultural biases that exist in standardized tests, for example, and although many have indicated the slight in these tests, many institutions still use them as objective indicators of success. Some institutions have known and unknown lists of banned materials that would give students viewpoints that challenge the status quo. To be successful in identifying and withstanding epistemic violence, you should be aware of the limitations of the educational system you are in. Walton[x] cautioned that students must "...change their expectations of the present system before they seek an education in that system." In other words, know what you are getting so you can better discern what is missing. It is most often the case that institutions will not have the faculty or staff diversity to counter a perceived inferiority of non-white educators that privileges Eurocentric ways of learning. It is also likely that seemingly objective traditions like the tenure process and the establishment of "classic" readings will inherently dictate who and what carries merit. The anti-Black propaganda in these cases is often difficult to detect because the terms used to justify Eurocentric dominance in academe are terms like "historical," "classic," or "objective." It is these bias-related norms that go unprotested because we are not trained to detect them. Developing a bulletproof pane in your perspective involves preparing for the onslaught of systemic tactics that assassinate intellectual curiosity and culturally-centered thought. Without such a guard, you are vulnerable to being held hostage by one way of knowing over another.

The bulletproof pane is at its core a protective shield from negative resistance in academia. However, not all resistance to anti-Black racism is negative. There are positive forms of resistance that allow oppressive systems to adapt and co-opt resistance for its benefit. A tinted glass pane is therefore to protect your lens from glimmers of progress that obscure your prospective. Oddly enough, progression on college campuses is often hindered by *progression*. People will make statements such as, "we have taken some steps in the right direction on this and we are in a good place. This should continue but I think we can now turn our attention to (fill in the blank)." It is like seeing a cake halfway cooked and removing it from the stove to bake cookies. Developing a tinted pane is about discerning when you are being asked to accept propositions that will benefit the current system, not shift it. This is vital to avoid the kind of tokenization that removes you from being effective in the cause you seek to address. It is also helpful for moving beyond awareness to action. Building awareness is a classic form of positive resistance, as it perpetuates the myth of institutional amnesia and assuages the guilt of dissonance without any concrete changes. Knowledge does not always stimulate action. For example, an institution can engage in research projects on the perpetuation of racist practices on campus without instituting any changes that would disrupt racist policies and practices. Institutions can create cultural studies programs to address a lack of diversity in curriculum, but house such programs in departments that are dominated by white ideologies. Institutions can make commitments to hire more diverse faculty, but hold those faculty to the same culturally-biased standards that perpetuates their current absence from academe. Furthermore, institutions can use the concept of time as a strategic hold, allowing their resistance to appear positive in the sense of allowing for continuous "work." A tinted pane assists you in looking beyond the surface of positive forms of resistance. It can also aid you in understanding that making time to wage resistance against your oppression and receiving little to no academic currency towards your graduation does not prove your intellectual inferiority, but perhaps sheds light on the inadequacy of the academy to fully acknowledge and credentialize all knowledge production. A tinted pane makes is plausible to also understand that inadequate responses on behalf of your institution do not always mean that the individuals there do not care about your success.

A Bridge Called Your Mind

Sometimes it is an omen warning you that oppressive systems will not provide the means for your liberation.

The third pane of the window is made up of two-way mirrored glass. This pane is reflective and transparent while also being protective. Earlier in this book I posed the question, how does one fight in, for, and against the system in order to create change and sustain life? The two-way mirror is the mechanism that allows one to work without being seen and to identify internal and systemic behaviors that must be changed. Let me be clear, identifying white supremacy is a dangerous endeavor. The fear of the other that is inherent in racist practices can cause systems and individuals to attack those who seek to change them. You will do well to not always be visible to the guardians of the system. Furthermore, in order to heal your self-identity in ways that actively disrupt anti-Black racism and epistemic violence, you will need space for critical self-reflection and analysis that sometimes is unnoticeable to others. Doing so is sacred and necessary because the journey you are on is particular and easily misunderstood. The composition of a two-way mirror glass allows viewing from one side and not the other. This is important because it is not a lack of awareness of the counter-narrative that perpetuates supremacy; it is the dominance and oppression over that narrative. Systems that are unyielding to change are well versed in silencing or removing those who attempt to force change upon it. To stay the course, the kind of critical self-reflection you began in chapter one is essential.

The fourth and final pane of the window is constructed of stained glass. It represents creativity, spirituality, and transformation. It is not enough to be critically conscious; you must also be creatively imaginative about what the world can be. Maintaining hope and a willingness to envision something new is the key to removing the ambiguity of your future. Stained glass is often used in the windows of churches or buildings of significance. It is often designed with multiple colors that admit light in colorful ways onto the ground below. Your stained glass pane is the protection of your hope and ability to project that hope onto the next generation. This does not require you to be religiously inclined. It is a spiritual exercise, one that connects your intellect, will, and emotions (soul) to service needed in the world. This final strategy is a tool for learning to sustain life in ways that do not demand it from others. Together the four panes give you a new window from which to shift your perspective and confront academic cultures that claim to be critically thinking and socially just, yet uphold standards, traditions, and epistemologies that maintain white supremacy and perpetuate anti-blackness. The actions you develop as a result of your critically conscious self-awareness become your Django praxis and bridges the gaps caused by epistemic barriers and racist modes of operation.

Chapter 3: Creative Courage in the Classroom

In the introduction of this book, I begin by confessing that I am an educator. However, I did not start my journey on this path. In fact my first degree is in broadcasting. I started college on the campus of a Historically Black University (HBCU), Central State University, before completing my masters and doctorate at a predominately white institution (PWI). It is the contrast that exists between these experiences that brought me into the classroom and centers of diversity and inclusion on college campuses. Indulge me for a moment and allow me to reintroduce myself.

My name is Kyra Tynisha Shahid. My first name can mean lord or light. Tynisha can be interpreted to mean life or the state of being alive and well; and my last name, Shahid, means one who gives their life for greater sacrifice. I grew up in Detroit, Michigan and as a child I spent a lot of time with my grandmother and her sisters. Well into my adult years, I can still remember the lessons they taught me; Lessons about courage, about being proud to be a Black woman and being proud of loving God. Each of them would tell me often and in their own way that I was great. They thought I was beautiful, smart, and rare. I believed them. When I enrolled at Central State University, I gained new mentors that saw the same light in me, nourished me, and challenged me to dig deeper in my scholarship. Yet, the ebb and flow of Black empowerment and Black disempowerment was all around me. Redemption songs were familiar to me, as I was consciously aware of struggles for Black liberation and freedom. Freedom, however, can sometimes mean having nothing else left to lose. It is often what is left when all that is yours is gone.

When I began graduate school, I often challenged and reimagined what freedom could look like. In a sense, I constructed my stained glass perspective pane in this process. I became determined that intellectual activism would be the charge I would fulfill. I did so, because I had witnessed so much spirit murder and the death of creativity in the classroom for both the teacher and the students. I remember days when I felt like I was losing my mind. I felt that way because I was constantly listening to lectures and reading books about social justice, inclusion, equity in education and respect for difference, however I was mostly experiencing and seeing the opposite on my campus, in my community back home, and nationally. What I saw was a sickening distortion of what knowledge was and a mental slavery that obscuring the light and greater sacrifice that was in my name. It is very difficult to explain, even now, because the method in which I write this book and the language it is in are both part of the violence that was causing my discontent. My scholarship is critically conscious testimony from a marginalized voice and discourse in academe. I did not choose the classroom, I was called there. My teaching is a work of heart that is deeply rooted in the redemption songs I hear in my spirit for every student who is searching for truth.

The first time I taught EDXC242: Anti- Black Racism and Epistemic Violence, I was overwhelmed with fear and excitement. It was like the feeling you get when you are waiting on a rollercoaster to take off; excited about the ride but fully aware that you have limited control over what is coming next. I began every class, as I always do: by setting the atmosphere. I circle the perimeter of the class, praying and inviting the wisdom of my ancestors into the space. I touch every seat, and think very intently about the needs of each student who will sit there and all that will enter the room with them when they arrive. I begin each class with a song from our class playlist, which includes carefully chosen songs that provide rhythm and cadence for the topics of the course. I do these things to help transform our sterile classroom into an intentional, organic escape room for engaging intellect and spirit. Sometimes while setting the atmosphere I hear in my spirit the need to adjust the lesson for the class and I completely redesign what I have planned. The time it should take to create and design the lesson never equates to the time I actually have before students arrive, so I can say with full confidence that divine intervention sometimes suspends and expands time in our classroom. I love teaching because it is transformative and every time I enter the classroom, something grows, changes, and shifts within me.

I created this particular class because I wanted to provide a place for healing and recharging for students who were experiencing anti-black racism and epistemic violence- even if they were unaware it was happening to them. I know personally and professionally that colleges have very little spaces within them where a student can go and heal their wounds and restore their consciousness in ways that are not inherently anti-black. I also know that the recent killings of unarmed Black Americans have not impacted the curriculum most college students are experiencing, thus for most part, the classroom serves as an escape from reality and not a laboratory to critically engage it. To combat this dissonance-building model, I proposed the class as an opportunity to examine media, education, and law as areas where anti-black racism and epistemic violence can be detected and discerned.

My classroom is an amalgamation of pedagogies, strategy, and creativity. I combine music, performance, writing, and art in ways that serve as a colander for sifting out the gifts that academia stockpiles from students by forcing them into standardized categories and placing rules and regulations on the ways they should properly receive and disseminate information in the classroom. Without fail, the first question most students ask me is whether or not my class is "hard." I laugh almost every time and then reply, "yes, but not in the ways you think."

What they begin to understand is that the class is difficult because it pulls them in directions they are not often asked to go in the classroom: inward. Each lesson tugs at their understanding of who they are and how that "self" relates to and impacts the world. I ask them how they know who they are, how racism informs who they are, and what knowledge they engage regularly that constructs all these meanings for them. They undergo a similar reflection to the one outlined in chapter one. I warn them that the process is difficult and that the presence of anti-black racism and epistemic violence that they find in their thinking may be different from what they expect.

Creative Courage in the Classroom

To this end, I offer weekly discernment diagrams as an opportunity for students to use any medium they want to process their discernment of their experiences that week. What the students are not aware of is that these diagrams become building blocks for the construction of their four-pane windows. Some students write poems that reflect what is happening both inside and outside of the classroom. Some draw pictures of images that came to mind during class. Others journal their thoughts alongside the thoughts expressed by various authors from assigned readings. In these discernment diagrams is the unraveling of thought and an examination of epistemicide from college students today. Five of their voices are featured here as a way to allow the reader to see a few examples of what was under their microscopes in our carefully crafted laboratory. It is our collective hope that their voices better prepare you, the reader, to conceive a curative justice that heals the wounds that epistemic violence leaves behind. The subsequent five chapters encompass our escape in plain sight (a Wakanda of sorts) where brilliance and intellectual discovery can be freely explored.

The next section of this book is made up of a collection of five sacred texts that are a product of each student's relationship with self, with one another, with the world, and with the divine. Each chapter is a "book" on their divine interpretation and a record of discernment as they explored anti-Black racism and epistemic violence as undergraduate students. Their voices are examples of way to engage Django praxis to speak truth to power. Their opinions do not necessarily reflect my own, or the majority of the class participants over the past two years. They are portions of critically conscious reflection and discernment that each person has decided to share. What makes these chapters sacred is not that they contain high academic rigor or demonstrate profound intellectual dexterity. These texts are sacred because they are genuine to where each student was on their journey. They wrote about readings concerning mass incarceration while loved ones were experiencing incarceration. They reflected on historical racism the night after a racially biased incident on campus. They returned home to the cities where Michael Brown and Tamir Rice were murdered and allowed a new connection in their understanding to emerge. Their works, while creative, are not abstract. They reflect real-time emotions, feelings, and pontifications. These students engaged the hard labor of seeking to emancipate themselves from epistemically violent practices, while maintaining a sense of self. The fullness of their work cannot be shared here because to do so would be to undermine the necessity of the two-way mirrored pane introduced in chapter two. As a result, the next section, Redemption Psalms, is a soundtrack

of sorts that accompanies and synchronizes with part one.

Creative Courage in the Classroom

Part II: Redemption Psalms

Emancipate yourselves from mental slavery
None but ourselves can free our minds
Have no fear for atomic energy
'Cause none of them can stop the time
How long shall they kill our prophets
While we stand aside and look? Ooh
Some say it's just a part of it
We've got to fulfill the Book…
-Bob Marley, Redemption Song

Chapter 4: The Book of Taylor

Written by Taylor Zachary

Internal struggle of becoming apathetic in the struggle. Balancing self-care/ separation from struggle & addressing/accepting the "necessity" of struggle. Cognitive dissonance of "Anti Blackness is not my problem."
The difficulty of reengaging in this subject matter & the emotional fatigue that comes with it.

As an EDXC242 student, I only completed two Discernment Diagrams in the 16-week course, one of which is featured above. In a way, I regret this decision. I know I felt overwhelmed by my own development, finding faces of myself that I had never before seen, or, at least tried not to see. I only survived, that spring semester, because I shared in the energy of other students who were struggling just as I. Despite being in a community of mutually shattered, tattered, and growing individuals, I notice, now, with peculiar clarity, that I did not have the courage to allow myself the freedom to admit struggle. I showed struggle, yes. My beard grew scraggly, hair unkempt. The emotional tone of my aura spoke in the key of somber. Yet, I could not admit these things and reveal a greater internal struggle. I guess I called myself an artist and justified my disposition accordingly. My mind, as did my room, became a space of words and worlds, entrapped by theory, ideas and identity.

During the course, however, I did not cease discerning. I wrote poems of sorrow and hope. I penned essays of unlearning and struggle. I fought myself against myself, exercising a willfulness to dismember my Spirit – especially if it meant rebuilding all the stronger. I do believe, honestly, the process of dismemberment was life-giving for me. I am humbly haunted by the memory of one poem. I wrote this poem sitting in the closet of my old apartment. I remember the night because I remember the silence. The posture of hovering hoodies contributed to the stillness of the moment. I could smell emptiness in the air.

The Book of Taylor

The poem was titled, *Black Boy Lost.* The first line read: If I die in closet, three days before discovery. The theme of suicide – a curious theme – lay heaviest in this poem, as I imagined the time between death and discovery. As I sat there considering what it means to feel life, I reflected on the paradox in the death of a Black body. I thought, "Perhaps, Christ is an example. Perhaps not."

In the time I spent alone, in my writer's room, caging my soul between the outstretched lines of college-ruled canvases, I saw myself pass away. I watched the body, soul, and spirit of a care-free Black Boy become an enraged corpse, lost to shuffling stubborn feet through the psychological torment of white supremacy. In the afterlife, mirrors restored my form. I found my body in a world of white space, the fly in buttermilk; stuck in the belief that I was, precisely, who white people told me to be, all the while knowing their story of me to be utterly impossible.

The Book of Taylor

Being alive during that semester meant living out the death I was expected to have. It meant dying from desensitization, then finding life again. It meant living to avoid another death by desensitization. It meant dying from self-understanding, shedding layers and finding faces. The former I embrace, the latter I fear. Yet, this perpetual death and resurrection felt all too natural. I had opened myself to the responsibility of sacrifice beyond a care for my own wellbeing. It was, in fact, my wellbeing that did not exist. That is what I believed the world had taught me.

My discernment diagrams showed death and taught me resurrection. Perhaps Christ was an example. Perhaps not.

I could not see beyond the circus of stress and emotional chaos masquerading as reasonably bright smiles and ambition. It is as if the university space encouraged students to cope with their stress by the guarantee of a return on investment. It seemed odd to me to observe my fellow students suffering through a lack of reflective time, especially since our institution embraces Jesuit values of reflection and discernment. Yet, I knew that most students hardly carry the words to describe what it is, precisely, that is affecting them. I learned that it is a privilege for a student to speak power to their present.

I once believed the greatest cancer to our university was a lack of education centered in Blackness. I thought it was unacceptable that ever semester I had strained myself to find a class to enroll in that would have a syllabus with at least one Black author, let alone a class taught by a Black professor. What student believes they have the time to dig through course catalogs to find such classes, which, by their scarcity, seem intentionally hidden? Not only would students need to know what it is they sought, but they would need to know why they needed to seek it and work quickly to enroll during the semester that the class is offered, since most of these courses are not considered core courses and/or are not offered on a consistent basis. Am I responsible for seeking these classes out? What role does the university play in creating my needle in a haystack adventures? Is this kind of epistemic violence a permanent part of institutional culture?

Perhaps this is too great a burden to place on the institutional culture of a university. In a space where time curiously revolves around the pivot point of four years, where issues and observations lose voice by the turn of a semester, one must wonder if the university space is ever meant to truly change. I suppose, when I say truly change, I speak of a change which does away with the necessity of perpetual critique of the lack of inclusion of Black intellectualism. How foolish of me to carry such an expectation! I think that the university mechanism is no less stubborn than the self-indulgent will of a child. Surely overtime they are bound to change; yet, their innermost guiding principles forever remain intact. I know that these institutions were not established to educate me. As a child transitioning into adulthood is complete with flaws, so too must our university indefinitely share the same condition. Forever do we raise the bar too high. I am always aware of the distance between the ideal and the actual.

Sometimes I pity our university – the child who just can't seem to get it right. Administrators arrive and depart, carrying their strength to love elsewhere. Faculty grows complacent in a responsibility to their discipline. Students must live in the present with an eye on their future, consenting to the non-actualization of their power under the 'what-ifs' of post-graduate expectations. It seems as though the students who work the hardest, emotionally and psychologically giving themselves up for the slaughter, are rewarded with the habit of false promises and debilitating debt. Yet, those students who drink four years into the memory of belligerent stories graduate from the business school with the tools to replicate undergrad into adulthood under the protection of a six-figure salary. Amidst such contemplation and turmoil, I and sixteen other students, sat in EDXC242 for sixteen weeks, realizing more and more that our 75 minutes was sacred.

It was as if, for the first time in my seventeen-year student career, I was valued simply for being present. No other course, no classroom, no professor has made such an effort more clear. When Dr. Kyra closed our classroom doors, we were no longer Xavier students tapping toes and eyeing the clock. Our chairs were cockpits at the head of an intergalactic space shuttle. With each lesson, we weaved in and between stars. I'd close my eyes and imagine that in a moment's flash, a student would poke her head out of the window and discover how oxygen exists in the unexplored pockets of her consciousness.

We were time travelers. We were imaginers. We were movie scriptwriters and famed poets. We were news reporters returning our doctrine to the ignorant people of earth. We shared space as co-anchors facilitating one another toward the essence of truth. We shared the goal of looking God in the face. On many occasions, we did.

We imagined ourselves beyond the limitations of our reality and returned to our reality with the lessons of our imagination – breaking the chains of creativity and overcoming the barriers of language. We had the freedom to put on our super-suits and step into those superpowers intentionally kept out of reach. It was as if we were waiting for ourselves to arrive. EDXC242 was the catalyst of homecoming. Only in this class did I experience the holistic values of a Jesuit Education. Because of the sacredness of our space, the challenge of the material and time to genuinely reflect on our process, EDXC242 embodied all that I desired my college experience to be. It gave me the space and validation to illustrate how, with pure sacrifice, the imagined can engineer healing into the actual.

The Book of Taylor

***

James Baldwin titled a collection of essays *Nobody Knows My Name* to damage assumptions about who and what the American Negro is supposed to be. The beauty of this title is its poignant accuracy. Even the name 'Negro' inflicted upon the Black-American body, no less dangerous than the racist assumptions linking the language together. Many names of a similar caliber have followed suit. Be the Black American merely a 'boy', merely a 'nigger', merely a 'negro' or merely 'Black', nobody knows our names.

In the opening paragraph of 'My Dungeon Shook', the famed letter Baldwin wrote to his Nephew James, Baldwin challenges his nephew to find his name. More immediately, he demands that he know who he is, or at least search for who he is, so as not to fall victim to believing what the white world says about him. For a man is only destroyed when he believes that he is what the white world calls *a nigger.* Yet, the problem of the *nigger,* the problem of the *negro,* is not the burden of the Black America. We bear its burden, yes, but this *nigger* – the idea, the necessity – is not our concern. Never have we clung desperately to the name *nigger.* Never have we etched our skin with the brand of Negro. The white world has often and always made us to believe we are who they say we are. The example is in athletics. The example is in marketing. The example is in movies. The example is in our schools, our classrooms.

But, we are not this *nigger* they dream of, nor have we ever been.

Some time ago, I needed to find my own name. This project commenced during the third year of my undergraduate study. I found and fell in love with the *Autobiography of Malcolm X.* I was primed to need Malcolm. I could not read *The Autobiography* and leave the book the same person who had begun it. No, this would have been absurd and, surely, I would have disappointed myself, as well as others who shared a stake in my political process.

Malcolm's honesty earned my captivation. If there be a spell in his work, it was the spell of honesty. If there be a spell in Baldwin's work, or in the tip of any poet's pen or the stroke of a painter's brush, be it honesty. And honesty, I believe, greater than any other literary device, earns captivation.

Looking back, I imagine myself as a single lifeboat swaying at sea, choked by the fumes of a sunken ship and lifeless bodies. Returning to shore would be less of a task for me, but the fate of gods. Only by submitting myself to the ebb and flow of nature, the push and pull of the waves, the strength or weakness of the wind, would I stumble upon survival. My path, though already written, could endure no authorship by the fingertips of my expectation. All that I could do is stay alive. And, even staying alive seemed too much a burden to survive the approaching storm. My body carries the legacy of two families and a multitude of generations. My first name is Taylor, named by my mother. My mother is the beauty of my life. She came close to death a few years before my birth; my presence on this earth is her gift from God. She never lets me forget this. A duty in life is returning to her the beauty she shows me, like a mirror reflecting the glory of Angels back to Heaven.

My last name is Zachary. I am still exploring the spiritual power of this name. I grew up with this name stretched across my back, on baseball Jerseys. I did not, however, understand the name which held my shoulders high. As a kid, I always found joy in being the last person called on in the class. I knew my place in line. On the baseball field, I wore number twenty four, inspired by my idol Willie Mays. In the classroom, my number was twenty four. Destiny always works herself out. When our third grade classes would line up for the water fountain, I would always be last. I mused about the old saying "the first shall be last and the last shall be first". There was something about my name that transcended coincidence.

However, Zachary means much more to me as an adult. As I am learning what it means to be my father's son, I am learning what it means to be a Zachary man. There is a responsibility woven into carrying a name, especially a name molded in purpose. My father's mother shows an example of the spiritual potential of the Zachary name. As I mature, I will continue to look toward her wisdom for guidance. My father, of course, is a man of purpose and distinction, never ceasing to remind me, by illustration and honesty, the history of the Zachary. As I grow into adulthood, the lessons of my childhood and the lessons of his own will become the building blocks of our foundation.

My middle name is Azi. Azi is a derivative of Aziz, one of the ninety-nine attributes of God in the Afro-asiatic languages. The Afro-asiatic languages are a combination of North African languages which carry a deep spiritual history. These languages are Hebrew, Arabic and Egyptian. Aziz means strength, power and perseverance. My life has been none the lesser, I have never, though, discovered myself until I discovered my middle name. For some time, I chose to identify as my middle name. A few friends who went by their middle names inspired me. Beyond their inspiration, however, I chose to identify by Azi because I need purpose in language. I needed a name through which I could discover more than who I had been and even, perhaps, who I was becoming. For two years, I only called myself Azi, dropping my first and last name.

I learned, however, that only being Azi is incomplete. The challenge of today is appreciating the synthesis of all of my names. My full name is Taylor Azi Zachary. I am still learning how to say my name with power. I am still learning how to articulate each syllable. I am still learning how to hear the name I bear. At times I feel burdened by the weight of my name, the power held within it. I cannot, however, run from something which is rightly my own. I cannot hide from who I am, nor is escaping fate an option. Perhaps the trial of self-misunderstanding derives from a rejection of my own truth, an unseeing of my name. By the presence of my own name, perhaps I am closer to myself then I know.

Chapter 5: The Book of Eseoghene

Written by Eseoghene Obrimah

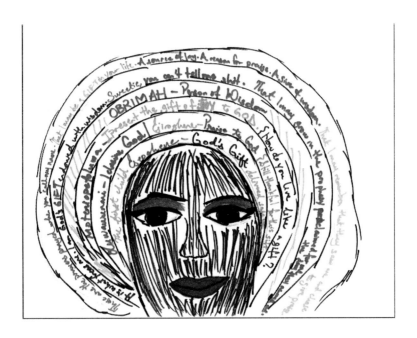

Greatness was prophesied in my life the day I was born. My ancestors, in naming me, set my life path. The image above is a visual representation of the meanings of my name, Eseoghene Oluwawunmi Ejiroghene Moteniopefoluwa Obrimah. Eseoghene is an Urhobo name meaning God's gift. The name given to a first child in thanks to God for safe delivery; but it's not just a prayer, it's a challenge and a prophesy. My name tasks me with being a gift to those around me, a resource to them. It's a hard thing to balance when it feels like your purpose is to be a gift, that is, something given to others. You also feel the need to reserve some of yourself for yourself.

Oluwawunmi is a Yoruba name and means "I desire God." Ejiroghene, Urhobo, means "Praise God." Moteniopefoluwa, Yoruba, means "I present the gift of joy to God." My name is basically a thanksgiving psalm in two different languages. It's a constant reminder of what I mean to people and my role in the world. When life is hard, when I feel my self-esteem dropping, I remind myself that from the moment I was born, I was considered a gift; I was a source of joy and a cause for praise. I am all that now and will always be. Obrimah is an Urhobo last name meaning "person of Wisdom." That is my family name; it's the blood that flows through me. I know if nothing else, I am smart. My knowledge has always been the trait I am most protective of. Nigerians are very concerned with the protection of the family name, thus, I constantly feel the need to ensure that people are aware that I am a person of wisdom.

My discernment diagrams demonstrate my ability to exist on the intersection of the theoretical and creative world; to understand concepts and be able to translate them into stories that resonate. They show me that I know and have known how to channel pain into creativity and translate knowledge to art. They tell me my purpose. Humans are usually left-brained or right-brained. The left side of the brain deals with cognitive processes that are analytical and quantitative. People who are left-brained are logical and detail-oriented. The right side of the brain is the creative side. People who are creative are more intuitive and look at the big picture. I lean right-brained. I am more creative than I am analytical, but I have an almost even balance between the two. My discernment diagrams show what exactly that looks like for me. The process of creating them showed me how I can allow both sides of my brain to work in conjunction to create stories that benefit the world. They are a visual representation of my journey towards discovering my purpose. A part of social justice work that is extremely important but is often overlooked because of how difficult it is, is defining what a racially just world looks like. My discernment diagrams tell me that I can imagine worlds that are just and where black people are flourishing. Take a look at my journey...

I mentioned earlier that my knowledge is the most important thing to me. A big part of me deciding to take EDXC242 was to expand my knowledge while simultaneously proving what I already knew. Two actions that don't really go well together. The first week of class, something was made very clear: in order to access the knowledge that I already had in me through my relationship with my ancestors, through my experiences, through my education, there was more knowledge that I needed to attain. In retrospect, in order to fully comprehend the impact of colonialism and white supremacy in Africa, I needed to understand racism and white supremacy in America. I'd been walking down a path and finally realized that there was a mountain in my way the entire time preventing me from fully accessing all my knowledge. However, the solution wasn't to try and get rid of the mountain. It was to be in relationship with it, so that I could climb it.

"Knowledge is Power."

"With great power comes great responsibility."

The Book of Eseoghene

So now I've acquired this knowledge and I know all these things but I don't know what is expected of me or what I am or what to do with it. All I know is that it's a lot. I'm like a newly independent country. I need to break out of a system that wasn't created for my benefit while creating one that is. The advantage for me, now, is that I know things, so I get to do this on my own terms.

There's always a really dramatic moment in superhero movies when the superhero realizes that their newly acquired abilities are actually really awesome. You see the emotion in their eyes change to excitement as the promise and potential of what is possible with their powers clouds all the fear that was just there. There is a fire that begins to fester when you realize that the power that comes with knowledge isn't to be feared. Now you need to figure out how to channel it. Superheroes get a suit, a shield, a hammer, vibranium. Dr. Frances Cress Welsing writes that black women are queen warriors and teachers (Welsing, 1991). It is through discovering your calling that you determine what tools you will take unto the battlefield.

THE ENDARKENING

    The realization of what is necessary in order to fully understand the world and who I am in it is difficult. If I avoid it, I could easily lose myself in all the knowledge.

That's how supervillains are made. At some point, rather than constantly looking for what's out there and how it can add to me, I had to curl into myself and understand my own purpose so that when I turn back to the world, I can give to it without losing myself.

SEEING TWO WAYS

I'm in a new environment that I don't fully understand or know. Carrying a new identity and everything that comes with it. But my family doesn't get it. This shouldn't be my concern as far as they're concerned. But this is my struggle. And my other struggle is tied to this. The National Community here will not see my entire being. The National Community there will think I dropped the being they made me in exchange for another one that, to them, is inherently criminal. And the global community will see a confused flake. I just tried to see it in my two ways. But sometimes the Black girl in America and the Black Girl in Nigeria don't get along.

The Book of Eseoghene

The Black girl in America and the Black girl in Nigeria don't get along and I need to figure out why and how to reconcile them. The Black girl in Nigeria doesn't want to be (or acknowledge that she is) Black and the one in America is dumbfounded at how dumb the Nigerian is. Who has something to gain by keeping the Nigerian girl and American girl at odds with one another? Why? Who told who what about the other? Why is it so difficult for them to find things in common with one another when they have everything in common with one another?

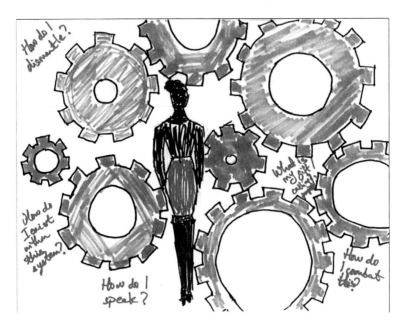

In understanding that there is a system that permeates everything, I need to figure out where I exist in it so that I know how to either escape it or dismantle it.

Pain will make you do things. Whether those things are good or bad is up to you.

Making the decision to do something with the pain rather than just letting it sit there is a vital one. For me, my pain fueled my purpose.

"Knowing who you are makes who you are worth knowing." – Dr. Kyra Shahid

Discovering purpose, knowing who you are, understanding the reason why the universe called upon you to exist at this specific point in time, gives you confidence. The confidence to turn around and look the world in the face and demand that it see you, know you, respect you. That confidence came from the analysis of and reconciliation with the pain of the past so that I could finally be at peace with the person I had become.

With self-consciousness comes an inability to avoid the healing you need to do internally as well as with the world around you.

The liberating power of self-definition and walking in purpose. The manifestation of the prophecies that were spoken into my life.

The Book of Eseoghene

When I reflect back on these drawings, I know that EDXC242 has completely flipped the lens through which I examine the world. It has forced me to engage with my past and critically analyze everything that I believed to be true. It's taught me how to analyze the present so as not to be fooled by what the world wants me to believe and find the truth in the story being sold. It's challenged me to imagine a future that is just. In the book Brainwashed, Tom Burrell writes, "Many of us have been conditioned to believe that whites are the pretty people, that their traits and physical attributes are more suitable than our ugly features" (p.87, 2010). I did not realize that I was Black until I was almost 18 years old. I spent 2 years before that arguing that I wasn't "really Black" because my blackness had not been definitive of my life experiences, and yet it had in the most dangerously subtle ways and EDXC 242 helped me realize that. I lived not realizing that I was Black, thus, I did not think it was a problem to devalue parts of myself attached to my blackness. That was the greatest form of epistemic violence. The devil you know is better than the devil you don't know.

I've found that a lot of Black people in the United States talk about going to Africa, the motherland. They feel that, in that space, they will be able to be themselves, feel that their natural attributes are beautiful, and that they will feel valued. The unfortunate truth is that white supremacy permeates every part of the world. It looks different everywhere, but it exists. You know racism, I know neocolonialism.

EDXC242 has impacted how I interact with the divine. I am a woman of faith. My race was not allowed to influence that. The sacredness of religion means that no other aspect of you can influence it, it should influence every aspect of your life. But why can't my culture influence my religion just as my religion influences my culture? Worship should be a reflection of our relationship with God. Our relationship with God is influenced by the way we live our lives and the way we live our lives is impacted by our culture; therefore, culture should influence on how we worship. A lot of the time the way we worship is defined for us. Who leads, who follows, who and what is holy and who and what is not are all things that the system has already defined for us. Through the imagery of white Jesus and male disciples, apostles and prophets, Christianity seems to be a religion created for the empowerment of white men. To be a white man or to be associated with one is to have a closer connection with God. In "Born a Crime," Trevor Noah writes about how his South African grandmother believed his prayers were more powerful because he spoke English (2016). This challenged me to think about why the way I experience life is not allowed to influence the way I experience God. I think about how neocolonialism has demonized elements of my being, my language, my culture so that even I don't think they are worthy of being in the presence of God. Meanwhile, European pagan traditions are practically indistinguishable from Christian practices.

I've had to realize that, despite the social connotations attached to my blackness, I am still fearfully and wonderfully made. The idea that I should suppress some of my wonder, my beauty, my magic when I go to God is an attack on my humanity and my identity as a child of God. It has been in the realization that I can take my entire self to God, not just parts of me that I've been told are acceptable, that I have been able to fully experience the love, grace and power of my God.

In reading scripture, I see the influence of epistemic violence. I grew up hating Vashti and Hagar based on how their stories were told. In Genesis 21, Hagar is portrayed to be a baby-bullying homewrecker. In Genesis 16, it is evident that she is a survivor of sexual assault and workplace harassment, but it's convenient for the maintenance of a certain narrative to prevent people from tying those parts together. We need to be hyper aware of how stories are separated, disjointed, rewritten and erased in order to maintain certain narratives. In Esther 1, Vashti is portrayed as disrespectful to the King's orders and is consequently banished from Persia. However, when read consciously, it becomes evident that Vashti wasn't banished from Persia because she disobeyed the King, she was banished because the King's advisers believed that if word got out of what she did, women all over the kingdom would realize that they had a lot more power than they were aware of and would refuse to be oppressed.

While growing up, I was fed a lot of stories about different people and I believed those to be the truth. I never took the time to evaluate what I was being told and try to put those stories in any type of context. That ended up affecting what I thought of many people: African-Americans, White people, the U.S. History, my country's history, the LGBTQ community, victims and survivors of sexual assault, Christians, Muslims, Vashti, Hagar, the list could go on. It created a single mindedness that I didn't even know that I had. When I finally decided to gain the knowledge that put all these things I thought I knew and understood into context, I realized that it's a lot harder to unlearn things than it is to learn them. It's a hard thing to handle when you realize that the truth, that your truth is incomplete or just a flat out lie. EDXC242 taught me how to deal with that.

The Book of Eseoghene

Chapter 6: The Book of Adrian

Written by Adrian Parker, Jr.

My name is Adrian Tyree Parker Jr., which right off the bat tells you that I was named after my father. When I step into a room of people that know him, my name signals that it is time for a mental comparison between the two of us. There are assumptions made and debates about whether we look alike or not. People are curious about whether or not I have the same disposition and most importantly, if I can sing as well as he can. Like the numerous sons names after their fathers, I had a choice to make about whether I would spend my life trying to be like him, trying to be the opposite, or just trying to find my own identity. When I learned early that the mental comparisons would be a common occurrence, I intentionally tried to distinguish myself from him. My father played football. I did not and chose to get involved in dancing and acting instead. I worked out so my body would look different than his and I made an effort to maintain an even-tempered, rarely rattled demeanor. I did not attend the same church as he did, and I only sang in church because I did not crave fame the same way that he did. As I have gotten older, I realize that living life with the sole purpose of being my father's opposite is a life where the decisions are already made for me. That life is not the one that I was meant to lead.

My nickname at home is AJ (Adrian Jr.). My family started calling me that at a young age to help distinguish me from my father while at home. That is how I knew myself and introduced myself to the friends that I made in elementary and middle school. But I realized that the nickname carried with it, a person. That person was a vulnerable and childlike which to me symbolized being stagnant by never growing up. After middle school when I began understanding myself, I stopped introducing myself as "AJ" and started introducing myself as "Adrian". I was less concerned about being compared to my father and had begun to grow spiritually. "Adrian" to me symbolized maturity and growth and getting to my desired place in life. Now, as I have gone through my college experience I am Adrian T. Parker Jr. One day there will be a PhD at the end of that but for now, thanks to EDXC242 I will settle for "the scholar".

In reading my discernment diagrams you will find a young man full of faith that evil will be defeated. At the same time that young man is unsure of how the defeat will come. Each diagram reveals how I was continually searching for answers and long-term solutions for overcoming anti-Black racism and epistemic violence while also being an advocate for love and reconciliation. At the beginning of the course Dr. Kyra asked us what we believed our purpose to be. From that moment my mind constantly tried to make the connection of how the class would help me walk in that purpose. Since EDXC242, my understanding of my purpose has shifted but this class was the stepping-stone necessary for me to reassess how I show up in the world. My discernment diagrams reflect this struggle and transition as I thought about my own experiences with the subject matter and how those experiences related to the course. In making those connections I was consistently questioning my role in "the machine" that is social justice.

Looking back now, I am able to see how that question actually meant that I really did not know what my purpose was or else I would have been able to answer it and dive into different questions. In the midst of this class I lost a close cousin, came to question and understand agape love in a different way, and reevaluated my relationship with God. I was someone that had so many voices telling me who I was and what I was going to accomplish that I could not hear God's voice or my own thoughts. This course put me in a place where I felt alone despite going through it with 16 other students. I do not think that was a bad thing either, because in that place I was allowed to question and understand myself better. I found my name reflection exercise to be the quick way of thinking about this identity process. In my name reflection, I noted who I was around family, who I was around friends, and who I was while away at college. In making those three distinctions I had to ask myself in which of those places did I feel like I was being most true to self. The answer was simple, all of the above. At every stage I felt that I was being true to self because that is where my growth took me. Today, my growth continues to lead me down the road of scholarship and combined with the work of my classmates that have gone through their own growth; I believe that anti-Black racism and epistemic violence can be overcome.

Entry 1 (Starting at Week 6: Diagram 5):

I was intentionally quiet on the subject of mass incarceration this week for one reason. My limited experience with family members in jail meant that I had a lot to learn. My uncle was an anomaly in our family from the standpoint that we have always done well enough that drug dealing did not have to be an option. My uncle chose to go down this path anyway. He didn't settle for being a small-time, on the corner dealer either but became a large dealer and even smuggled drugs across the border. When he was caught he went away for most of my childhood and did not return until late in my high school career. Upon being released he turned his life over to Christ and because he is so dang smart he has found ways around his criminal record prohibiting from finding work. Between real estate and other small start up businesses he has received loans from banks and found investors, which has all resulted in him doing very well for himself. This is not the narrative nor the reality for most African-American males caught up in the criminal justice system in the United States. This is not to say that it cannot be but I am acknowledging that it is not. This is why I decided to just be quiet and listen this week as my classmates shared the familiar narrative that our authors explored in their chapters. As someone that had the "overcoming despite all of the odds narrative" instilled and engrained in me by my family I needed to take the moment to realize not everyone can say the same. The next step is deciding what I can do with the information I have been given practically as I move forward into education so that the norm can be broken before it even starts in the lives of the students that I come into contact with.

Entry 2: On Isis Papers:

February 21, 2017

I do not even know where to start this week thanks to you having us read from 3 different authors. I guess I will start with Dr. Welsing and her argument that it is on black women to turn the tide of the African-American male population. I feel that it takes all accountability away from black males and completely devalues the role played by black male figures active in their households. Most likely my contention comes from that fact that I am a black male but that is okay. No one appreciates having their future is dependent on someone else and while sometimes they may not have the choice, I do not believe that this instance is one of those times. I mean after all it seems like the entire book is centered around the black male genitalia, so it is only right that I am given some control in stopping that affliction. I will end my rant there.

What I found quite interesting about this chapter was the part where Dr. Welsing calls on black women to stop referring to their sons and lovers as "baby." I found this statement particularly interesting due to a conversation I had with my boss last week. I was in the middle of making a decision to not go to Paris this summer. While trying to make this decision I expressed the fact that my mother felt that I should go because the opportunity presented itself for a lot cheaper than it would in the future. When I mentioned this, my boss, a white male, sat up in his seat and started to ask me about the type of relationship I wanted to have with my mom. He asked me whether I wanted it to stay where it was at, meaning me being her baby and her getting to make decisions for me or whether I was ready to initiate the beginning of what would be me taking a respectful step into adulthood and friendship. Taking this question into consideration with what Dr. Welsing said, my mind was blown that my boss had this mentality and I did not. I do not know whether that is just from my own experience or whether this is something felt all across the black male experience. If it is something that is felt across the black male experience then I would really like to see the way that it has played out in more people's lives than my own. This idea makes me think about the way black males praise their mothers in popular culture, a specific example being Tupac's song "Dear Mama." Despite having a step-father who was a member of the Black Panther Party he still viewed his mother as being on a sort of throne. It just makes me wonder in what others ways this ideation of mothers can be seen throughout black culture.

Something else that Dr. Welsing made me think about was my obligation to my race. If black women have the obligation to teach me the way to view myself and white supremacist cultures, in what ways then do I owe it to black women to date within my race? And that is not something that I necessarily believe but it is something that I questioned for just a moment…at least until I remembered that if you're doing life right then you can't control who you love. It does warrant further reflecting once I think about the situation with Eden however. In what capacity could a black male figure play in this entire scenario (because as far as I was informed there was not one involved) and how that would affect the way that Eden responded. Is this what I subject a black woman to dealing with on her own if I were to marry another race or would that actually be beneficial in possibly educating another race. Things that make you throw up your arms and go "aw hell."

From Michelle Alexander I was upset because for the longest time I have been waiting on the argument for Affirmative Action. I have a classmate in PPP that has attacked Affirmative Action any chance that he can when we talked about race in class. Initially I was appalled that no one had ever mentioned this argument before until I started getting into the depth of it. I realized that there is no way in hell a civil rights activist or intellectual would bring up this argument when it mentions everything that is wrong with Affirmative Action. Despite the fact that it really just wants a better system, the same way that Republicans claim they want a better form of Obamacare. It makes no sense to me that this conversation is not being had more amongst intellectuals and activists. Why are people not doing more to capitalize on the one piece of legislation that we have? If you're going to give us something to keep our mouths shut then at least do not half ass what you give us.

In thinking about the machine that I mentioned a couple of diagrams ago, there are so many parts to this damn thing that the hard part is figuring out where you function best. It is not overwhelming by any means to me, if anything it gets me excited because I do not want to only do one thing for the rest of my life. This realization helps me fully understand what you mean when you say that you are trying to work yourself out of a job. I have no idea what my concentration will be in the future when I go in to curriculum development but whatever it is I don't want there to be a need for it by the time I leave my position. And I understand that as I move on to my new role, the old techniques and approaches that I used may no longer be applicable and I will have to cater to my customers. (That is the genius behind places that allow their consumers to customize their items).

This class is contributing to me in more ways than I could have possibly hoped for coming into this semester and I am thankful for every second of it because I know that it is not only for me but for everyone that I come into contact with from here on out. And I recognize that advice and ideas will continually change but that is what I am looking forward to the most. Adaptability is what I used to pride myself on the most and this class is the ultimate test of me actually being able to adapt in terms of how I approach certain conversations with different people and being able to talk and understand others when I enter a dialogue with them. Now, with that being said...

Why do you this to me? 'I Am Not Your Negro' caused all kinds of feelings within me but I will say that the thing that stuck out the most to me would have to be the struggle with the faith in white people that James talked about dealing with. He said that he was different than the other three men mentioned in the regards that he did not hate white people nor was someone who stood out there and protested against all the wrong doings, but he had a different role to play and he played it. This internal struggle is just an illustration of one of the things that I focus on a lot which is role and purpose and playing that role to the best of your ability. I think the struggle when working towards reconciliation is something that all conscious black people have to make a decision about. They have to decide whether or not it they want to have the faith in white people to help accomplish this or whether they just want to say "forget it" and be bitter as they continue to live their lives in a way that they believe is defiant to the white supremacist system. That is something that is difficult to work past if there is so much anger built up inside as we witnessed from the way the talk show class period turned out.

Entry 3: Hate Rising, Get Out, I am not your Negro

Between "I Am Not Your Negro", "Hate Rising", "Brainwashed", and "Get Out" I have taken in too much anti-Black racism and Epistemic Violence in a week's time. There is nothing that really describes being in a place where you are equally disturbed and satisfied learning about all the systems of oppression against Black people and how it plays out in the world in so many forms. I could not be more thankful for the opportunity to not only learn about the structures but also learn about ways to tear those structures down. The argument about the way racism has launched one of the largest and most successful marketing campaigns in history has added yet another lens to the camera that I see the world through. However, I have a major point of confliction with Tom Burrell and his small critique of the role that music plays.

While I do think that he has a point in pointing out how hearing something over and over again plays a role in the psyche, I do not possibly see that you could fault music in accomplishing what it is meant to do. From my understanding, music is a form of expression that (in an ideal world) talks about the various realities that are faced by the artists that perform them. In this regard I am not sure that it is fair to blame music for perpetuating self-destructive behaviors when this is in fact what artists, especially artists of color, experience in their daily lives. And I am not naïve enough to think that some artists and record labels do not create their own narratives to sell more records but at the very roots, songwriters have had some contact with what they write about. The question for me then becomes would it be feasible for music to consistently be about "wanted realities?" It goes through phases, especially the rap industry, of dreaming about the future, but can that cross over to other genres of music and not be about monetary success or what else society has attached to what it means to be successful? Or does it even matter because at the end of the day if actions are not taken then does it really matter what the music is expressing? We can sing, rap, and dance to songs that talk about having a cohesive family unit but how can we go out and make that reality when many of us do not even know what it looks like. That is just something I have been meditating on recently and I do not want to make this nearly as long as last week's so I'll leave it there.

Entry 4: How do we get people to listen without violence because they'll "listen" and nothing will change?

One of the questions that I had in mind after hearing from Ms. Evans was: in this current political climate what do you think the approach should be? She mentioned being a Malcolm X follower instead of a Dr. King follower because she believed that the non-violent approach was wimpy. She also mentioned that the way you get what you want is by kissing butt and everyone knows this. Lastly, in addition to those statements I also thought about what she said about us continuing to repeat our past mistakes and that she is 70 years old fighting the same battles that she did years ago. I do not want to be in the same boat when I am 70. My question about the approach takes those three statements into account and makes me think that without violence then people aren't going to listen. But as people of color we always have to worry about our appearance in society and proving to people that we are not the savages that they believe we are. It begs the question should we even worry about that if at the end of the day it means that someone will listen? But we think back to the many riots that have happened in response to the mistreatment of our people and it can be argued that eventually they were listened to...but then what? Everything went back to the way that it was. An approach, a response, a strategy that bares fruitful results. An approach that appeals to the powers that be while also allowing us to get our message across without being lost in the approach. Measurable goals, sustainable goals, goals that achieve more than the past without aiming too high (as defined by us). Goals that can be attacked from all sides. But how do we get those goals listened to and who accomplishes these goals or determines when the goals are reached as generations and leadership pass and along with them their different standards?

Entry 5: Long term strategies & goals to combat the Black Inferiority (BI) campaign #Longevity is key

Brainwashed has been an interesting read in this course. I think in comparison to the other books while just as valid in some points we critiqued this one more than the others. Dr. Welsing shattered our worlds but gave us a new framework to think about anti-Black racism through even with the arguments that we felt were outrageous, Marc Lamont Hill made us emotional while critically analyzing how our communities got to this point, similar sentiments came from Michelle Alexander, and then we reach Tom Burrell who provides a marketing/advertising frame of mind that we can definitely see pieces of in the world but we are more critical of his argument. I do not know whether this can be attributed to us growing more comfortable in our identities and knowledge or whether we just really do not like the fact that he continues to blame the black community for perpetuating the BI campaign. Regardless I find our critique of Burrell to be fascinating.

It did make me think more about long-term strategies and goals. Thinking about the role that your class plays to educate black people about themselves and their history in the most necessary of ways in conjunction with what is that we are going to need to address campus culture going forward. What are the ways that we can maximize the empowerment of black students while also fighting for social justice so that it is not just 17 prominent faces around a PWI in this course trying to bring our learned knowledge to other spaces? How do we also be mindful of the fact that you want and are called to teach other classes? But then also being mindful that we are students first and so to ease the load of fighting for justice we need to do better having long-term plans and goals so that we do not have to sacrifice our grades in order to stay on top of our campus administrators and faculty. So while I do not agree that propaganda is actually the most effective component to combat racism and the myth of black inferiority, I do agree that there is a lot to learn about the longevity of such a campaign and we should be thinking longer and harder about such plans for ourselves.

***

Ever since taking EDXC242, I am constantly thinking about my purpose which I now know is to fight for social justice in the classroom as a professor and scholar. No longer do I have the audacity to just go through the motions of life. Of course, I am only human so there will be days when I am just not feeling it or I am exhausted because I did not get enough rest the night before. But it does not matter because I cannot stay down when I know I am called to create and educate. With this on my mind all day and every day I find it difficult to go to classes that do not feed into my purpose.

Undergraduate study requirements appear to be trivial and I feel like I am wasting my time when I sit in classrooms that ask the same questions that were asked 1000 years ago by Plato or Aristotle. I am all for having a baseline understanding to build off of but we should have moved on to different questions by now. EDXC242 has made me forward thinking but not in every subject. I am forward thinking when it comes to rethinking anti-Black racism and epistemic violence. I view core classes that do not address these issues and help me move towards reconciliation as a form of epistemic violence. While I am wasting time in a core class I could have been in another class that gives me the information that I am looking for.

126

The Book of Adrian

EDXC242 has made my major classes important in a different way however, because I have a new lens to receive the information from. Now I am able to read Machiavelli or Spinoza and apply their works to the struggle for liberation, love, and reconciliation. I now see the connection between Bacon's Bensalem and Marvel's Wakanda and how they both are examples of the way in which a utopia struggles with keeping its own people believing in their way of life while also trying to decide if they want to spread their way of life to others. My thirst for knowledge has never been greater and for that I cannot thank Dr. Kyra enough. My collection of books has expanded greatly since taking EDXC242. Books are scattered in my room, car, book bag, and saved on every piece of technology that I use. When I found out that information was being withheld from me I could not help but continue to search for it. New ways of thinking that come from an Afro-centric point of view are critical to me at this point in my academic studying because all I have been taught from the white male Euro-centric perspectives which do not connect to my inherent spirit which is African and indigenous. My journey continues and because I am a scholar that will be always the case. I loved books as a kid but school sucked the joy out of reading for me; thanks to this journey I have rekindled my love for reading and learning.

Chapter 7: The Book of Diamond

Written by Diamond Brown

My name has a lot of meaning behind it so trust me when I say that I grew into that meaning over the years. Most people know that a diamond is a precious stone consisting of a clear colorless crystalline. I however, am not colorless. I'm a walking contradiction, both diamond and Black, but I think I'm the most beautiful thing that ever existed. I am the piece of black coal that didn't crack under pressure but instead grew stronger, more brilliant, and bolder. I have had my fair share of pressure and pain but through it all, I shine brighter. My parents named me Diamond because it perfectly describes me.

My Discernment Diagrams tell a story about my journey over the timespan that I was in EDXC242 and my feelings about many events that happened during that year, both locally and nationally. Some of them have nothing to do directly with what we were focusing on in class that week simply because my state of mind was not reflective of that. I was glad to have the space to be real, to be authentic, and to be present. The discernment diagrams were a way for me to express my emotions in the best way that I knew how, through writing poetry. They tell of the heart ache I experienced and of things I became aware of due to the course amongst other things. My discernment diagrams were my outlet and allowed me to express myself and my feelings in a way that made sense to me.

As I reflect on what I've gained from this experience, I realize that I became far more aware of the ways that epistemic violence and anti-Black racism were present in my life and in the lives of those around me. In this realization, I began to challenge epistemic violence and anti-black racism through my other course work in other classes. While other students wrote about technology's place in our generation, I found myself addressing issues such as the mistrust of the American healthcare system by its Black citizens and the origins of where this mistrust stems from. I began to recognize that my friends who had been unable to return to the university because they could not afford the increasing tuition rates among other issues, were byproducts of a system affected by these issues. While I always knew that the retention of Black students was an issue, I never knew what to call that issue, or understood it as intricately until after this course. Things that I always knew were a problem became clearer as to why they were a problem. I found myself questioning a lot of things that I thought I knew and understood. This new found knowledge was at times overwhelming and exhausting to say the least. It was as if someone showed me something that was there the whole time just out of sight but once I saw it I couldn't unsee it. In not being able to unsee these things, I understood more clearly the issues that were present in my life, at my university and in the world.

The Book of Diamond

As I reflect on the experience, I feel that it is difficult to explain what happened in the course to people who were not there with me. It was eye opening and challenging in more ways than one. I hope the poetry you read hereafter gives you a glimpse into my personal journey.

1/19/17

Hill put into words
The deaths I had seen on Tv.
It hurt even more seeing them,
Written on white paper in black ink.
These chapters laid the truth out,
As simple as could be,
Made it clear the truth wasn't simple,
And that the next nobody could be me,
Or my best friend,
Or cousin,
Or even a stranger walking by.
Which doesn't make it better,
And still leaves me wondering why.

Can I touch your hair?

So this white girl asked me
"Can I touch your hair?"
Immediately I thought
Didn't you hear a seat at the table?
Did you hear what Solange said on track 9?
DON'T TOUCH MY HAIR, means no hands on this holy
shrine
Is it not enough to admire this crown upon my head?
Are you not content with gazing upon these gravity defying
locs?
Why do you wish so badly to entangle your fingers in these
curls?
What satisfaction will this bring you
Are you willing to get to the root of it all?
Too see how deep my pain runs?
To feel theses coils and know they are coiled around one
another
Because if they don't protect one another who will
Because they just like black people only got each other
Because they like black people are tired of being told how
to live
To be straight when all they've ever known to do is curl
and bend
Because they've finally learned to be content with who
they are
And I'll be damned if you put your hands in this hair when
I just got this far
Not to mention this twist out is bomb and took too long to
do
Like my friends know better than to touch it and if they
can't then who are you to?
Do you see all of that when you see my hair?
But I know the answer to this question is no

The Book of Diamond

And I know the ignorance is too great and the education comes with a cost
A cost I cannot bare to pay today
It cost my energy and my time, my patience
Honestly how can I give them this when I have none to spare?
But I didn't say any of that
Instead I simply smiled and said
"No, I just did it"
And I can't even say that with too much grit
Because everyone knows if I do, 1st thing they'll holler is that angry black woman shit
But Solange wasn't lying when she said on track 6
We got a lot to be mad about because it's hard being a Black chick
But again I said none of this
Instead I gave a simple answer
Because that's all I could bare to say
See I've grown tired of my culture being stolen
And my features being commodified
My people being judged about their features while they're praised on others
So this, though small
Was my act of resistance?
I've grown too tired
Too weary
Too exhausted
To explain why it's a problem
Why it's rude and uncalled for
So I simply say No
And sometimes
I don't even have the energy to do that.....

Give Me Liberty

Give me liberty.
That is all,
There is no OR.
No alternative.
No death.
For Life & Death is in the power of the tongue
And I will not invite such a thing into my life.
All I ask, is to be given what was promised to me since
birth,
The principles this country was founded on,
Not the actions.
All I ask for is equal opportunity
To have the freedom my ancestors never had
The opportunities they were never afforded
Give me liberty in every sense of the word,
Allow me to pursue my happiness,
With my nappiness,
With this Black body,
As a women.
Allow me to live as I am,
And not be persecuted because of it.
Give Me Liberty!
This is not a request,
This,
Is a demand.

The Book of Diamond

Onions

If I peeled back the layers
What would you find
What would you say if I told what's in my mind
Would you cry?
Like when onions layers are peeled back
When I told you the struggles of being both woman and
black?
Please do tell exactly what you might do
If I told you of all the things I had to swallow and not chew
All the things I nearly choked on because I couldn't quite
stomach it
Do you think it would send you into a raging fit?
If I told of all the things I had to stomach and hold down
inside
If I explained each one in detail would you run and hide?
Would you listen perhaps to my story or tale
Will you keep your eyes open when I remove your veil?

The Book of Diamond

<u>Did I lose my mind or find it?</u>

I've lost my mind.
Could you help me find it?
I seem to have lost it,
My mind? I think it was…
Was it in my bag?
Way down at the bottom?
Where'd I leave it last?
I recall a film, or 2 or 4 or more
That I saw
Maybe I lost my mind there?
Like a thought when you walk through the door
OR maybe it was one of the countless conferences or
symposiums I've attend
Perhaps I left it behind in one of those rooms?
OR it could be in my classroom, where I've learned of
Epistemic violence & anti-black racism
I could have left it in one of my books for that class
Like a bookmarked page I can't seem to find
I cannot seem to recall where I saw it last
Could it be in my fits of rage
OR possibly my stream of tears
Maybe I left it next to my heart
That was filled with both hope & fear ?
Was it that summer night I cried myself to sleep
After another black body was gunned down
It's funny really,
In a dark way I suppose
How in the knowledge I gained
In the insight I acquired
I lost my mind
Or maybe I'm just beginning to find it

The Book of Diamond

My hood ain't no hood

I lived in the hood
But it never seemed like a hood to me
It was home
A street of mostly family and friends
A community strung together even in times of struggle
See we lived in the middle of the street
Uncle bug lived down the street to the left
 RJ was across from our house
and peaches lived next door to Papa with Ms. Washington
Pappa lived two houses down from us
He stayed home & took care of Mama
Let my cousins
Uncles,
And Auntie live there to get back on their feet
Mr. R lived across the street from him and them kids better
not be on his lawn
Phatter and Keke lived down the street the other way
Zek lived across the street and always came over to hang
out with Bruh Bruh
Carlo & Ant did too
My brothers weren't all brothers by blood, but they were
still family
I remember walking to the park with Papa & Des
Where some my fondest childhood memories were made
So, when a girl in my class, who never stepped foot in the
hood
Who knows nothing of it
Says that the hood is dangerous
That it doesn't do any good for those in it
Says that the hood is a wasteland
& says it with disgust
not upset with the system that created the issue
but with the people who suffer its consequences

The Book of Diamond

I had an issue with it
The problem with the narrative of the hood isn't that it's
completely wrong
It's that they never paint a full picture
They make ghettos out to be graveyards
They forget the hood is somebody's home
Forget there's community, even within the chaos
The hood is no utopia but it's some folks' reality
& they make the best of it
They took the neighbor out of neighborhood
& Gave us the second half
But if I'm being honest
I knew more neighbors in my hood than I've ever came to
know in my suburban neighborhood

The Book of Diamond

Soda cans & get away cars

When people are driven mad
Driven insane
We question their actions
Question why they are the way that they are
But we forget to ask who the driver was
Who took them there
Or at least paid the cab fare
And sent them over the edge.
Have you ever thought
Maybe they're trying to escape
Trying to get away to a safe haven
Maybe it's their getaway car
A psychotic break
to get a break from reality
I've heard it said that when a soda can explodes
And burst from the pressure inside
We blame the force that shook the can
Not the can itself for exploding
So why are people any different?
Maybe sometimes people don't choose to take this path
Don't choose to burst at their seams
To be ripped apart
But rather they're shaken until they explode
From the sheer pressure that's built up inside
And maybe sometimes the force is a person
And sometimes it's a moment
Or a single word
Maybe sometimes they're not the driver of the getaway car.
Sometimes we have soda cans in cup holders of getaway
cars
And all it takes is a push,
A nudge
To hit the gas

An uncontrolled acceleration
With no brakes
only breaks from reality
Causing the can to shake until it explodes
sending the car right off the edge

The Book of Diamond

Respectability politics

Your Respectability Won't Save You
Won't grant you no peace
Cause you could still get shot walking when Black in these streets
Still get stopped and frisked by police
Still get told what you should or shouldn't be
So let's give the respectability politics a rest
As if you're on a better than them quest
Because at the end of the day we're all still black
And when you're Black in America there's a target on yo back

Battles Worth Fighting

I told my father that I can't win for losing
To which he replied
"So why are you fighting a battle you cannot win?"
I did not have a response
Instead I thought about what he said
Why fight a battle you cannot win?
And I had no simple answer to this
Because sometimes the battle aren't worth fighting
Sometimes you get beat up just to find out there was no
point
No small victory
That the sacrifice was in vain
But sometimes…
Sometimes even if I know I'll lose
At least I'll go down swinging
At least I can say "I didn't go down without a fight"
And when I do get knocked down I'll get back up
Because I know that the battle is worth it in the grand
scheme of it all
So yeah sometimes the battle aren't worth fighting
But every now and then we come across battles that are
Even though we know we may not win.
Sometimes you have to lose a battle or two to prepare to
win the war.

The Book of Diamond

Close to home

A Man was killed
Shot dead in the street
And there are no words to make it better
Make it less sad
Less heart breaking
And I will leave it at that
Because I do not wish to make the death of this man live on
forever through my words
Would like to grant this family some rest for their souls
What little it may be
Though it makes it no less permanent
Perhaps it allows it to be a dull ache in the years to follow
With one less reminder
Rather than a piercing inescapable pain
There are no words I can offer for this tragedy
For this family.
So instead
I offer my prayers.

Description:
This poem was in response to a specific shooting that
occurred. It's intentionally vague, to avoid the continuation
of the story being told in a way that would cause it to
remain vivid in the mind of loved ones. It is to both avoid
reopening the wounds of this man's family as well as to
acknowledge the countless number of individuals lost to
gun violence.

The Book of Diamond

Chapter 8: The Book of Sequoia

Written by Sequoia Patterson-Johnson

My name is Sequoia Egyptia Patterson-Johnson. I've been asked what my first name means, but never my middle or my last names. In pursuit of this information, I called my mom and asked her a few questions. According to the wonderful Ms. Patterson, knower of all things, Sequoia means strong. My mom said that she saw the name in a book of baby names, and she researched the name. When she researched the name, she saw that my name is derived from Sequoyah, the Native American chief responsible for creating the Cherokee syllabary, or scripted language. My mom said that when she heard the name, she felt her soul reverberate (her exact words) and she just knew that Sequoia would be my name. She hadn't been looking up any girl names prior to this, because, as the knower of all things, she swore she was having a boy.

147

The Book of Sequoia

My mom says that she liked the philosophy behind the name. Chief Sequoyah was a genius, he was one of the strongest (both physically and mentally) Native Americans, and he was very creative. He was regarded very highly by his tribe, and because of his work the Cherokee tribe literacy rate quickly surpassed that of the nearby European settlers. My mom says that she named me Sequoia because the name signified greatness to her, and that's what she wanted/wants me to be: great. I also googled this, and it checks out. The name Sequoia (spelled the English way) can also mean sparrow, and it's also the name of the world's largest tree species. This had nothing to do with me being named Sequoia, though. The tree is a coincidence, but it makes me feel kind of cool sometimes. I'm also not named after the car, which is an important distinction for me to make. I was named after a chief for a reason, not a tree or a car or anything else that might be named Sequoia.

The Book of Sequoia

My middle name is Egyptia, which I never tell anyone because I don't really like it. It doesn't mean anything, and to me is a little ghetto. It also has nothing to do with Egypt, so basically somebody put a bunch of letters together and was like "Yeah, that'll do." When I asked my mother why she chose that for my middle name, she said it was one of the middle names of one of her spiritual leaders. She liked the way it sounded, so she passed it down to me. Joy. When I googled it, I learned that Egyptia is the name of a videogame *Battleworld*, but that's got to be recent because I've googled Egyptia before, and that didn't come up. I really hope that's recent because if my mom seriously named me after a videogame *Battleworld* with mutant humans, I'm fit to be tied. It's one thing to have a ghetto middle name (my mom says she's not ghetto but her "ghetto side came out with that one", her words again) but to have an intentional videogame middle name? That's not okay. Like, that's going to show up on my death certificate and obituary, and what will people say? She must have loved video games, poor thing? I'm not here for it.

I have two last names, Patterson and Johnson, which in this case means that my parents weren't married when I was born. My mom actually wanted to make Johnson my last name, but my biological father wasn't there when I was born so the hospital wouldn't let her give me his last name without at least hyphenating it with hers. Patterson is my mother's last name, which she inherited from her father, who inherited it from his father. It was my mother's father who played a significant role in raising me, so I always felt like a Patterson. That was my "dad's" last name, my mom's last name, and my grandma's last name. Patterson is our family name, it's who we are. I didn't even know that my last name was hyphenated with Johnson tacked on at the end until I was in eighth grade and had an assignment requiring me to look at my birth certificate. I didn't really care, but I thought it was weird that my mom let me live for thirteen years without knowing my own full name. Anyway, when I asked my mom what Patterson meant she said that it must have been a slave owner's name that got passed down to one of our enslaved ancestors, because the only Pattersons we know who aren't related to us are white. When I googled the name, it came up that Patterson has Irish, Scottish, and Northern English origins and means son of Patrick.

My second last name is Johnson, which I inherited from my biological father. I don't really feel like a Johnson because I didn't know it was my last name until a few years ago, and I also didn't meet my father until I was sixteen so there were no other Johnsons around for me to feel connected to. My dad's last name used to be Catlett, which he inherited from his mother. When he was around eight or nine years old, he and his siblings were removed from his mother's care and placed into the foster system. My father was separated from all of his siblings, except for his same-aged cousin whose last name was Johnson. My father thinks he was put under file as a Johnson so that he and his cousin wouldn't be separated. I don't think my father has ever seen his birth certificate to confirm this or not because he's never had to use it. He was on the streets for a lot of years, and he's only ever worked under the table. My father is also unsure of who his father is. It could be some guy with the last name Catlett who he says he briefly remembers, but it could also be his cousin's dad, the Johnson guy.

I don't have any nicknames, really, besides Quoia and my older sister on my father's side calls me Coy, which I only let her do because I don't know her well enough to say that I don't like it. She's trying to be nice, and I appreciate the effort because it's pretty awkward to live as an only child for so long (she was twenty-two and I was sixteen when we met) and then boom, new relatives. I don't like Quoia very much either because if you're going to go all the way to say Quoia you could just add the Se part too. It's one syllable, but people think it's endearing so I don't protest. Growing up, my mom refused to let anyone nickname me because she believes that there's a lot of energy and respect tied into a name, so it should be said fully and with intention if it is to be said at all. I didn't really care, I just thought that Sequoia is a hard name to shorten in a way that doesn't sound silly and/or phonetically pointless. Anyway, that's my name. It's long and unique, and employers probably know I'm Black just by reading it on paper, but I like it nonetheless.

The above introduction of myself is from a discernment diagram I wrote for EDXC242, when I was asked to reflect on and flesh out the meaning of my name. In all of my discernment diagrams, I was asked to reflect on and flesh out my interpretations of various things, primarily concepts that I had never before been granted the space to process. This being said, when I reflect back on all of the discernment diagrams I completed for EDXC242, I recognize that I still feel overwhelmed sometimes by the way this world that's supposed to be mine is structured. I feel like I was catapulted into something I didn't ask for, and I don't always know what to do with that feeling. On one hand, I know that I should be grateful to be alive and to get to experience the sweetness that this life has to offer me. But on the other hand, all the bitterness, and pain, and hate, and fear feels like too much to navigate through, and I get mad that I have to do it and show up in the world like I'm supposed to be here.

It's hard, sometimes, to be proud to belong in a world that was structured for my systemic extermination, be that physical, spiritual, educational or mental. It's hard to be proud and grateful when my world, the one I have been catapulted into, screams to me that I am un-human, and that my very existence is problematic. My Blackness, to this world, means that I am angry, and ugly, and invisible but for the negative preconceived notions that most people associate with my Blackness, all the whilst my humanity begs for me to be happy, to be beautiful, and to please, just please, be seen for the soul that lies within my body. The anti-Blackness in the spaces I occupy make me feel erased in every sense of the word most days, and the violence imposed upon my intellectual development causes me fear and anxiety, because if the system refuses to teach me what has been, how will I know what is to come? These are the feelings I had when I entered EDXC242, and these are the kinds of questions I left with.

Nonetheless, I'm glad to have learned what I did in the class. I have always felt like I knew there was more than my teachers were telling me about, and I was often reprimanded for suggesting that what I had an idea of was valid enough to be spoken aloud. This happened so often for me that I became afraid of my own intelligence. I was afraid to be smart and knowledgeable, and I began to feel like my mind was an incurable and inescapable burden. Being invalidated repeatedly was exhausting, and I was losing my will to keep being tired. But when I took this class, after my first week there I felt valid for the first time. And I felt valid in an educational space that costs tens of thousands of dollars to be in.

So, even though I was and still am overwhelmed to have begun gaining the tools necessary to analyze the world that recently became mine, I do not resent my knowledge. I do not resent the journey I began embarking on and which I am still committed to traveling on. I don't feel like I have "the answers," but rather that I have even more questions than when I began this expedition. And I'm okay with that now because I know that there are spaces in which, and people with whom, I can ask those questions. I know that when I open my mouth in pursuit of truth that I will be embraced instead of scolded, and that the heaviness I feel in my heart is not in vain. I know that it's okay to have anger, and hurt, and resentment, and apprehension, and distrust because my intuition is just as real as I am and God gave it to me for a reason.

I have also come to know that the reality that I call mine is not okay, and that it's okay for me to say that. The name I was given tells me that I'm bigger than the box I was put in, and that I will continue to flourish no matter how hostile the environment. The heights I am destined to reach tell me that it's okay for me to look and think so critically that it exhausts me. And when it does, I take naps, I eat more Starbursts than any sane person would ever recommend, and I learn and grow, freely and unapologetically, because I can and because I have to. That's what I know about myself today, because of where I was then. I know that I am committed, that I am brave, and that I am enough. Here is a small look into the journey that brought me here:

Discernment Diagram: Entry 1

This week we learned the functional definitions of anti-black racism and epistemic violence, and began reading Nobody by Marc Lamont Hill. The definition for anti-black racism left me feeling somewhat conflicted because we learned that every human being is of African descent because Africa is where humanity originated (which I knew) and that to claim not to be of African descent (so any other racial identity or ethnic identity) is inherently anti-black because it results in a sense of othering and distance from Africa itself and its obvious descendants (the more melanated people of this earth).

The definition for epistemic violence was so intricate and complex that it alluded to all the ways that epistemic violence and anti-blackness are embedded into nearly every aspect of society, and it made me feel sad and kind of defeated. Not defeated in a "I'll never make it or be able to do anything to change the world" kind of way but I felt so tired after our first couple of classes. I want things to be different and I feel like I'm going to exhaust myself trying to go about making them so, and I don't want my spirit to be killed in the process. These definitions made me more aware of how deep the oppression really runs and how deeply it affects the people who fall victim to the systems constructed to keep 'others' down.

When reading *Nobody* earlier this week, it hurt so bad it felt good. It was nice to see that someone else feels the way I feel about the occurrences in this nation and to be exposed to new information that align with my observations, but it's heartbreaking to read these words and know that they are true and have been for hundreds of years. It's hard to read about how so many lives have been discarded just because they were lived under the poverty line and in brown skin. And in class the next day I heard about all the ways my classmates and professor have felt like nobodies and have seen their family member and friends treated as such, and it was hard, but in a comforting kind of way, to hear that so many of my peers feel just like I do in some way or another.

I'm not sure what this all means in terms of my purpose, but it definitely makes me want to work harder and achieve more so that I can be seen as a somebody to the system of nobodies that I've been catapulted into. Class on Tuesday gave me this overwhelming feeling that I HAVE to be somebody one day for my dad, who was forced to assume the role of nobody for far too long just so he could put food on the table to feed my mouth. On Tuesday, and for a while now, I've felt like I can't let his death be in vain. I have to be somebody and carry out his legacy in whatever way that I can. And that's probably too much to take on, but I think something in me needs to do it. I'm here for me but I'm here for him too, and for the "us" he left behind. I think it's the only thing that keeps me from feeling utterly and indefinitely defeated, even as I'm learning such heavy information in this class.

Discernment Diagram: Entry 2

Tuesday, January 24th, 2017: Today in class I spoke a fair amount, which is kind of unusual for me, so I was proud of myself today. And it was easy to feel proud because last night I delved nose deep into a book that allowed me, finally, a sense of validity. As a class we read The Isis Papers by Dr. Frances Cress Welsing, and I feel different after reading it, like a flower that finally has the courage to bloom. All of the things my elders have told me about, and nearly all of the things I felt like I saw but leaned to never speak out loud, can finally be acknowledged as valid.

I got quiet in my early teen years, not because I didn't have anything to say, but because I was often reprimanded for daring to speak the things I thought. When I was younger, I must have said things that not a lot of other people said, because I got sent out of class a lot, and it wasn't because I was talking to my peers when I wasn't supposed to be. I got sent out because I asked my teachers questions about concepts they wouldn't allow themselves to ever truly consider.

It started happening my freshman year of high school, when I was thirteen. The first time, I was asked to remove myself from science class because I suggested that the human origin is in Africa, because that's what science has offered us, with the discovery of Lucy, the oldest human fossil. I got sent out of the same class a few days later because I asked, if Pangea were still connected, would Africa be at the center of it? And wouldn't Ethiopia, where Lucy was discovered, be at the very center of the earth's land mass? And things usually start in the center and move out, so couldn't all humans really have come from Africa? I got sent out of a history class once because I suggested the early existence of the Moorish people who civilized, and soon after offered education to, the early inhabitants of the Caucus mountains. I even took a low grade on an English paper once because I wrote about why slaves were forbidden to read, and how ignorance is a token to oppression.

I have been, time and time again, by more than just one "educator", denied fair access to my own education, solely because I dared speak of a truth that I refused to be kept ignorant of. This continued to be my experience until I finally forced myself to accept that I could not try to engage my education with my process of enlightenment, because the two were unfortunately incongruent. I remember how confused I always felt after that. And how angry it made me; to stifle my voice just so I could keep the opportunity to learn in the schools to which I always paid tuition.

I didn't have anywhere to feel this, though, so I got quiet. I learned to stop telling people, namely my instructors and my peers, what I thought about because I had grown tired of watching their eyes get big right before their mouths formed words of mockery and invalidation. I got tired of having to wonder if I was crazy for believing what my elders taught me, when that always felt like my version of right. My mother laid pieces of the Color Confrontation Theory in front of me when I was twelve, she just didn't tell me what book it came from. The following year, my grandmother taught me about Sarah Baartman, and my grandfather, a former Black Panther, explained to me his theory about the "War on Drugs", aka the War on Black, and how mass incarceration factored into this.

It didn't stop there, though. I did research the best way I knew how, and I watched documentaries while most of my friends were giggling over sitcoms. I was young, but I knew that there was something deeper to learn than what the State of Oregon deemed necessary for me. I just didn't know what it was all the way, because I didn't have a place outside of home to ask all the questions that kept me up at night, or access to the information I hoped would one day quiet my mind.

And then, last night, I read Dr. Cress Welsing's book, where she lays out white supremacy and how it stems from a sense of white inferiority, and all the different forms this has taken on, and how deeply it has affected people of color. I thought about all the ways this has affected me throughout my short time on this planet, all because I didn't know that the lies were just myths that caused my truths to be denied by those who didn't know either. And then, after shooting off sensible theory after theory, Dr. Welsing said that she wrote this book so that people of color can know, and make sense of their experiences of oppression, so that the generations to come after us do not have to follow suit with the black man's plight, and be stifled out by the weight of white oppression.

I think this book, for this week at least, has made me aware of what I feel my purpose to be. Maybe I can be another someone to educate the little black and brown children that will soon walk the path that I am currently on, so that maybe it will be easier for them than it has been for me. Maybe I can show them how to see, when they're ready, the illusion of their inferiority upon which their education system is largely based on. I think that with the right tools and people, I can help build strong children, so that there are not as many broken men in need of repair.

This reminds me of one of my favorite quotes by Anaïs Nin, where she writes, "And the day came when the risk to remain tight in a bud was more painful than the risk it took to blossom." Just when I was beginning to blossom I

162

was told the sunlight I needed wasn't real, so I tightened up and went back to being just a bud, too afraid to try to blossom again. And it almost drove me insane, to be so quiet on the outside, but to have such a loud mind. This week's readings have, in large part, confirmed my views and led me to realize that my mind is not some illness to be rid of, but rather something to be cherished and allowed to blossom openly, freely, and unapologetically.

Discernment Diagram: Entry 3

This week my mind feels too full and, too exhausted to process deep thought. I can barely see the lines of this Word document because my eyes are too tired to focus, and watery from my constant yawning. After learning about this world's antiblackness, I feel kind of tired, like I'm misplaced in exactly the right spot. Kind of like the rose that grew from concrete. I feel like the tree that grew from concrete, too big for the environment set for me. And now I'm starting to see why I was even put in concrete in the first place, because I'm coming to know more about who put the concrete there. It's like my roots are reaching deeper than originally intended, rupturing from the toxic concrete that got poured over me.

I am a Sequoia, the world's largest, oldest, and fastest growing living organism, more powerful than some dare imagine. Sequoia trees, named for the great Native American chief Sequoyah who invented the Cherokee syllabary, never stop growing. And they can live to be 3500 years old if humans don't bother them. If you take an aerial view of the forests in California and Southern Oregon, you'll see that sequoias tower over all the other trees, all alone, just them and the sky. They're so tall that their height often goes unnoticed, because they're usually too big for the human eye to capture at ground level. Sequoias are strong, and can even survive forest fires, resisting significant damage from the heat of the flames and regenerating themselves to repair whatever minimal injury occurs.

I am more than what the world intended for me to be. I'm a black girl, born to a crack addicted absentee father who left me for another man to raise, and to a mother convinced that better didn't exist. I had fires to grow through from the jump, so that's what I do. I grow, and learn, even though it's less than pleasant sometimes. And I bet the only reason I think it's even okay to grow is because coming up, my mother always told me that my brain was too big for my britches when I frustrated her, but she always told me to keep growing, even when she didn't like it. I'll be sure to shout her out for that when I deliver my TED talk, or whatever it is that I'll do some day.

I think that's where I'm at this week. When I read The Isis Papers I feel like concrete got poured over me, and that all the nutrients I need to grow is really hard to get. So much is set against the black man and woman, but sequoia trees are highly adaptive, and can survive almost anything. So even though this is heavy, and my roots could use a better nutrition, I'll never stop growing. I'll get close to the sky, so I can look down and see how to block the concrete so that all the other trees can grow to their full potential too. I will grow tall enough to speak to God Herself, and I'll even do it in public.

Discernment Diagram: Entry 4

This week the class was assigned to read chapter 15 of Dr. Frances Cress Welsing's The Isis Papers, chapters 3-5 of Marc Lamont Hill's Nobody, and the first chapter of Michelle Alexander's The New Jim Crow. Our position paper, addressing one chosen question concerning anti-black racism and epistemic violence, was also due this week. I wrote about how race should be discussed in classroom settings, stating that not doing so is harmful because it allows room for ignorance. In the readings this week Dr. Frances Cress Welsing told us that we as black people, need to wake up and stop resisting white supremacy in futile ways. She wrote that unless we do not see where the fight and reform must occur, we can never understand the status of our own oppression and therefore never truly be aware of it. If we are never truly aware of it, we will only continue to be oppressed, and the cycle will continue indefinitely.

Marc Lamont Hill informed us of how today's legal system isn't centered around justice, but rather economic efficiency and resource conservation which in turn leaves many racially and socioeconomically oppressed persons in the dark about the legality of their persecution processes. As a result, many people plea guilty to crimes and go to prison for long periods of time, usually for minor offenses that should have been tried in court but weren't. He then writes about gun laws and how the right to possess weaponry stems from white people's fear of persons of color. In the last chapter we read, he discusses mass incarceration and how persons afflicted by poverty, mental illness, and other undesirable perils are cast away to prison cells. Michelle Alexander, in the first chapter of her book, connected the dots from slavery and its abolition, to Jim Crow laws and their legal elimination, to mass incarceration being a modern-day embodiment of both.

This week has been busy, and a lot of work has been required of me in this class and in each of my other classes. It makes me wonder if this is my midterm week, since most classes don't announce midterms they just smile, administer exams, and pile work on students. What I've learned this week in class, though, makes me feel less sure of my purpose. If legal systems are corrupt and due process is rarely implemented, should I set out to educate youth to keep them out of prisons, or should I look into reforming the prison systems and the legal processes (or lack thereof) that land so many people in prison to begin with? Should I be trying to spread gun awareness and gather with community members to try to prevent more liberal gun use laws from being passed into office? If I feel like my purpose is to help people see and know, do I just do that? Because then I feel like I'll only be trying to keep young people out of prison, and not actively trying to address the issue of mass incarceration and the numerous injustices that occur in precincts, courtrooms, and federal prisons. I know I can't do everything that needs to be done, but if I don't right now I feel like I'll only be addressing one cause and one effect while ignoring all the others, and that doesn't feel right.

I guess this week, other than feeling overworked, I feel conflicted and confused. After reading about mass incarceration and how deeply corrupt it is, I'm angry that it's okay to treat people this way and that it's so easy to just throw lives away. And I'm not just angry because it happens to other people, I'm angry that it happens to people I know too. Last week I found out that my little brother is going to prison, and he's going to be there for at least eight years. This week I didn't just read about what happened to other people who share my ethnic identity, I read about what happened to my little brother, the hardheaded little brown skinned boy I never liked but always dearly loved.

So, this week I feel conflicted and confused, because where do I fit and what am I supposed to do there? I want the prison systems to change because now I've got somebody dear to me there, and I want the school-to-prison pipeline to cease to exist because it didn't have to make my little brother its victim but it did. I want gun laws to be more restrictive, and education to be more well-rounded, and for black people, young and old, to learn to see their oppression and understand where it comes from so that it doesn't keep trapping so many of us. There's a lot that needs to be done, and I know I can't do everything but I also know that I can't do nothing. So which is mine to make different, and how do I know that part is the right one for me? And how do I know it's the right part for them too?

Discernment Diagram: Entry 5

After reading chapters one, two, four, and five of Michelle Alexander's The New Jim Crow, I see two things that I can say directly affect me. I could probably say a lot of things in this book do, but these two stuck out to me the most. The first is the introduction of crack rock to black neighborhoods in 1985. My biological father (not the man who I call Dad) grew up in Berkeley, California where crack was a big issue. When he was around nineteen years old, he started smoking crack, and thus suffered a near thirty-year crack addiction. Both fortunately and unfortunately, he walked out on my mom before I was born so I was never subjected to the perils of his addiction. He had two other kids, though- my older sister and my youngest brother- that don't get to say that for themselves. At the individual level, I grew up not knowing the second person responsible for my existence, nor that of two of my three siblings.

I also have a few other family members that dealt with crack addictions for considerable amounts of time. I have aunts and uncles that went to prison for a while for possession of crack, the distribution of crack, and quite a few males that were involved with my aunts and cousins in jail for domestic violence charges that result directly from crack abuse. My local community, northeast Portland, was known as "where all the crackheads be." A lot of my neighbors, friends, teachers, and coworkers' families have been disrupted by crack abuse and incarceration because of some form of involvement with crack. Tons of kids, including myself, have stories about waiting for the city bus on their way to school in the morning and being harassed by crackheads.

At a national level crack, has infiltrated communities, torn apart families, and led to the even further demonization and criminalization of Black men and women. It also serves grounds for the justification of meritocratic arguments suggesting that poverty and oppression are not due white supremacy but rather to individual laze and drug abuse inclination. On a global scale crack makes America look less like a desirable place to be. We imprison people for long periods of time behind crack, and a lot of people are pushed to the brink of desperation and try the drug or become involved in its distribution, and thus end up in prison or worse.

The second theme mentioned in the book thus far that stands out to me is in chapter five when Alexander writes about the absence of Black men in the home and the illusion that stems from this. The majority of black men absent from their homes are presumed to be lazy, immature, irresponsible deadbeat dads when they're often times victims to the "justice" system executing the War on Drugs resulting in the mass incarceration of black and brown men and women. As a result of this illusion, as young kids my god brother and I often heard black women (including our mothers) say that good Black men don't exist and that all black men are "dogs." My dad wasn't in prison but he wasn't around, so I thought he must have been a bad person. I grew up convinced that I was half "bad" and that my brother was going to grow up and become bad one day, because that's what I learned that Black men were. It was conflicting, too, because I didn't want my little brother to become one of the "bad guys" I always heard my mom complain about, but I didn't know yet that it didn't have to happen. This really affected my younger brother, who knew that he would one day grow into a black man that would inherently be "bad." He never unlearned these negative thoughts about himself, and was convinced that he could never be more. He gave up on himself a few years back, and now he's on his way to prison, suggesting that there's a deep cycle resulting from the illusion of Black male inferiority that feeds Black men to mass incarceration.

The absence of Black men and the widespread illusion of their status of inferiority has also affected my less immediate family. Out of my mom's whole family in Oregon (like 20 plus people) there are only three adult men not in prison, addicted to drugs, or absent from their families lives. Two of my cousins, and my cousin's husband are the only adult males left. Because there are really only women in my family, a lot of the myths about Black men that we (the kids/younger members) hear are rarely debunked solely because we don't have the opportunity interact much with Black men. According to a lot of the women in my family, aside from our cousins, all the Black men in our family- our fathers, uncles, and brothers- are "violent and/or drug addicts." This just further perpetuates the negative impact on Black male's self-image, sense of self-worth, and sense of self-efficacy that land so many in prison to be "disappeared" to begin with.

This also affects my local community. There aren't many Black people in Portland to being with, so there especially aren't very many Black men. Portland, before the gentrification started, was six percent Black. Now it's only two percent Black, and a lot of that two percent are women. A lot of my friends growing up didn't know their fathers, and a lot of my friends either had fathers in prison or brothers that went to prison. The only Black men we saw on a regular basis were either the neighborhood drug dealers and gang members, or our teachers. A lot of my male friends growing up often talked about when they would go to prison and how they would defend themselves when they got there, because prison seemed like an inevitable occurrence for them.

Nationally, a lot of people in the U.S think Black men are bad people because a lot aren't in their homes raising their kids, and the status of Black male imprisonment in often unmentioned. Black boys all over the country grow up feeling immense pressure to be "good Black men" in a world of "ain't shit ass niggas", or they don't even think it's possible for them to be good men. As a result, a lot of Black men resort to crime because of necessity, but also because they've been conditioned to think that nothing better is out there for them. Globally, Black men are perceived as negative members of society who should be behind bars, and are often regarded with fear and disgust.

Side note: Today in class something Adriana said almost made me cry. Like, I had to stop talking for a moment and pull myself together. She said something along the lines of "I'm just one person and I'll never have any power to change anything because who's gonna listen to me? No matter what I know, it's not going to serve me any real good because nothing is going to change." And I responded to her kind of aggressively, which I'll apologize for when I see her next week. She probably thought I was mad at her, but I wasn't mad at her I was mad for her. And maybe I took what she said the wrong way, but it made me so angry that a young woman as smart as her doesn't think she has any power. She could be monumental one day but she doesn't seem like she believes it, all because she's been conditioned not to. Today I think I saw nobody-ness in effect, and it broke my heart a little bit to see it so clearly in another person.

I used to think that I didn't have any power for a long time because I thought that I didn't matter. And because I thought I didn't matter, that I was a nobody, I accepted all kinds of wrongdoings at my expense solely because I didn't think that I deserved any better. I didn't know who I was and I was afraid to try to be somebody, so I gave a lot of my power away to the wrong people for a long time. I didn't think I could ever change the things that made me angry, so I accepted my oppression like it was always supposed to be mine. And I'm only just now starting to unlearn this. So it was hard today to see that someone else thinks this way about herself too. It was hard to see hope not be there, even though I know hope is hard to have.

It made tears well up in my eyes because I'm so tired of seeing young people so bright and new to adulthood already feel defeated. I think that's what I want to be able to say I did after my time on this earth is over, that at least one young soul didn't feel so defeated. That at least one person's hope wasn't crushed before they hit twenty because they knew who they were and what they could do. I want to be able say that the psychological perils of white supremacy are no longer strong enough to convince anyone else to hold themselves back. Today in class I just kept thinking about how I didn't want to ever again hear a young person say what Adrianna said, and if I do, I don't want to watch their face fall in disbelief like hers did today. I don't want to keep making room for learned helplessness, because it's not okay.

Discernment Diagram: Entry 6

Two people that I consider to be distant mentors to me are John Lennon and India Arie. The first one is a dead white dude, so he fills the first requirement for being both not alive and not sharing my ethnic identity. The second is a living black woman, so she fills the second requirement for being alive and ethnically identifying similarly to me.

I don't really know a whole lot about John Lennon, I've just heard a few of his songs and seen a lot of memes with his quotes on them. I know he was the cofounder of the Beatles, and that he was very wise. He was very anti-war and pro peace, which I think is what I like most about who he was. Or who he's been depicted to be, because who knows what's really true about celebrities. But I like his peaceful rebellion. He stayed true to what he believed in, even though it pissed a lot of people off. President Nixon even wanted Lennon deported from the U.S because he openly opposed the Vietnam War.

Lennon, in a lot of his videotaped interviews, talks about love, and peace, and happiness, and how to value the beauty of humanity and the interdependence on which our survival relies. I'd like to think that if I was alive in the 60's and 70's I'd be in the streets during protests waving around burning sage to clean the chakras of our nation with a megaphone yelling about how we should all just love one another and be as happy as we can under a capitalist system that profits off our collective misery. In all reality though I'd probably be attacked by police dogs while angry white people pulled my afro and called me obscene names.

I think John Lennon, though, is why I detest wars, mass and systemic murder, and standardized education. I heard this quote by him, and he said when he was 5 his teacher asked him what he wanted to be when he grows up, and he said happy. Lennon's teacher told him he didn't understand the question, and he told her that she didn't understand life. I dug that. Sometimes I don't want to be a doctor or a psychologist or an education reformist. I just want to smile and mean it. I don't want to hate anyone, or think about anyone hating me, or think about how it's so easy for us as a collective to casually erase life and steal people's joy. I want to have Bed Peace one day and be okay with it.

I grew up listening to India Arie, so I think that's why she feels like a mentor. Her voice is like water, and she sounds like that live even when she's been singing for two straight hours, so that's dope. But what she sings about, it makes me want to always listen. In the intros and outros to her albums, she pays homage to her ancestors and the artists that came before her who paved her way. She sings about brown skin, and how little things bring her joy, and seeing God in the people who've captured her heart. She sings about how there's hope even when it doesn't feel like it, mother's intentions for their sons and daughters, and how all over the world the ghettos all feel the same. In one song, India's Song, she sings that she was sitting under an oak tree when a strange feeling overcame her, so she took out her guitar and asked "Is this the tree where my brother was hung? Is this the ground where his body was burned?" She goes on to say that she wants to go to a world for her-where her shame is gone and she's free to just be.

India Arie lets her spirit come through her songs, and her art is so profound to me because it doesn't sound like she sings to people. It sounds like she's singing to God, whoever she perceives that to be. She doesn't deny or mask her spirituality solely for the comfort of mainstream media, and she's got the courage to sing about all the things I generally don't say out loud because most people's eyes get

174

big. She's very aware, but I don't think she lets it make her angry. She seems so peaceful and genuinely happy, but it's not an oblivious kind of happy. I think India Arie has that Black Girl Joy that I'm still trying to figure out how to master. She also looks like she smells like cocoa butter and clean sheets, but that's impossible for me to ever know without being arrested or something else equally as unfortunate.

I thought about India Arie when I watched Hate Rising yesterday. I'm not sure what she'd say to me if I asked her what to do or feel, but India's Song kept looping over in my head. Sometimes I just want to go to a world that's mine. I want to drown my shame and hear the wind calling my name, but instead I open my bedroom window to hear white kids passing by calling each other "nigga" and laughing if off because they've got the ignorance and privilege to casually do so.

Discernment Diagram: Entry 7

Last night I saw the James Baldwin film "I Am Not Your Negro" with a few of my classmates, and I have not been so angry after leaving a movie theater in a really long time. I should probably be saying something about the readings we did this week, which were powerful and resonated with me. But last night there were several times throughout the movie when my eyes weren't dry. After watching the film, I think it's safe to say that James Baldwin was a deeply angry man, and it is this deep ridden anger from which the beauty of his brilliance originated. Near the beginning of the film, an excerpt from James Baldwin is read, where he speaks about Medgar Evers,

Malcolm X, and Martin Luther King Jr., all of whom never saw their 40th birthdays. James Baldwin was good friends with the three iconic men, and when they were murdered, the paradigm of his world shifted and got darker than it already was.

In the film, Baldwin states that one of the main reasons that he did not return to the United States for so long is because he could not bear to witness the pain and sorrow in Betty Shabazz's face, or to watch Coretta Scott King forced to raise her children alone, silently missing her life partner. He said that he couldn't stand to see Medgar Evers' little girl smile, when Evers himself had been so brutally robbed of ever experiencing such tender joy again. And even though we were only 10 minutes into the film, my eyes stayed teary from then on because I think I knew what Baldwin meant. And at that moment I understood the magnitude of the sacrifice that these three men had given, both for and at the expense of their country of origin. Malcolm X, Martin Luther King Jr., and Medgar Evers didn't just sacrifice their lives. They sacrificed their children's' fathers, their wives' husbands, and their mothers' sons, and they did so readily for the advancement of our people and the recognition of the status of our humanity, which still has yet to fully be achieved.

When James Baldwin said what he couldn't bear to face from the families of these men, I became silently enraged, because the sacrifice these men and their families were forced into was not an easy one. And I know this because as my own father approached his last days on this earth, he was reluctant to leave me behind. When the scene played, I thought back to that day in the hospital. We were all there- my grandma, my aunt, my uncle, and myself when my dad's doctor came in and explained his treatment plan to him. And we all knew what she was saying, but we didn't want it to be true just yet. When the doctor left the room, my dad turned to my grandmother and asked what it meant, and she told him that it was over. If he sought more treatment it would only kill him faster, and that it was over now. After nine years, there was no more fighting to be done. At that moment I excused myself, because I refused to let my father ever see me weep, especially not for him. A few moments later, when I returned to his hospital room, the door was closed but I could hear him sobbing. I'll never forget what I heard him say. "I'm just so sorry. I'm so sorry. When her momma brought her into this world I held her in my arms and promised that I'd never break her heart. I'm sorry it's not true. I'm so sorry for dying. I'm just so sorry." And I'll never forget the way his eyes squeezed shut when the door finally opened and his eyes met mine again, because he wouldn't let me see his tears fall either. And I'll never forget what it felt like to hear a man apologize for his own death.

Anyhow, with that being said, I know that it's not easy for a man to leave his family behind when the life is stolen from his body. Medgar Evers, Malcolm X, and Martin Luther King Jr., and countless other black men who never got to turn 40, were forced to break their families' hearts. They were forced to sacrifice the core essence of their humanity just to prove that it was even real. They were stolen from their personhood just to that it could one day be established. And I can't help but think that if they were more than just "niggers" in the eyes of their oppressors, would the burdens of their premature deaths not had to have been carried on the backs of their young wives and children? If White people did not so desperately need to make them "niggers" would the shouting of their names be received by an answer instead of eerie silence? At the end of the film when James Baldwin asked, "Why do you need me to be your nigger?", I wondered why such indefinite heartbreak is still not enough to make theirs' whole. The blood of my people did not ever need to be shed to prove the status of their humanity, and such pain never needed to be plagued upon their livelihoods. And maybe that was the point of the film, so that people would finally declare "No more!", and refuse to ever be anyone's Negro ever again. That's where I'm at this week, even though I spent a considerable amount of time today talking about genetically recessive humans.

Discernment Diagram: Entry 8

This week has been a rather interesting one. I'm coming back from spring break, and initially I had a lot to do this week and I was overwhelmed. I was supposed to have two tests, three quizzes, a big paper that I didn't know how to go about writing, and an outline due for another major paper along with some other stuff all due this week. It turned out though, that I only had one test and a major paper outline, so my week has been a lot less stressful than I anticipated. I also just got the internship that I really wanted for this summer, so this week has been good. I feel like things are falling into place and that my purpose is gradually becoming more and more clear to me, which is very reassuring.

Today in class we talked to a woman named Barbara Evans, a white lady who was very involved in the Civil Rights Movement and the Black Panther Party. She even had a baby with a Black Panther, which at the time was extremely controversial. Race mixing, as she called it, is controversial even today. People from both sides shoot dirty looks and make snide, nasty comments at white girls dating black men and at black women dating white men, and this is today. Back then, it was literally life threatening for Evans and her son's father to be seen together with the small child. She and her young son experienced racism on various occasions in a lot of different places in the country, and Evans was forced to raise her son alone in order to assure that he'd live to be an adult.

This wasn't all that she talked about, though. Evans talked today about poverty and the notion of generosity, marriage, cultural acceptance, and the sense of belonging that she has felt with the black community since she was just eighteen years old. Barbara Evans made a lot of interesting points today while speaking to the class, but two stuck out to me the most. First, she said that racism was, is, and always has been, a white problem because decent white people have failed tremendously to educate other white people who lack their same decency. This was unusual to me because it often seems like racism is placed on the backs of people of color solely because we fall victim to it, but are not the perpetrators of it. That being said, it has always seemed odd to me that people of color are expected to educate white people about the origins and effects of their racism when it's THEIR racism. If I got shot, it wouldn't make sense to put me in gun control classes, when I don't even own a gun. It would make sense to put my shooter in gun control classes, because they obviously need the instruction for the weapon they possess. So Evan's comment today made a lot of sense to me, because it really is not my issue even though the struggles that come from it are mine to bear, at least for now.

The other thing she said was that it was our responsibility to not let racist comments go unchecked, but I think she said that because she assumed we were all white. That being said, though, as a person of color this made me feel funny because it seems like it is my responsibility to not let racist comments go unchecked. I feel like I have a duty to educate ignorant white people about how not to be explicitly, and sometimes even implicitly, racist. And it's a duty that I have come to strongly resent, because it's a burden that I don't feel I should have to carry. It feels burdensome that I feel a responsibility to educate my peers when I'm in an institute of higher learning with professors that could easily pick up this slack if they wanted to. I don't think it's my responsibility everyday to educate people on how not to be racist or how to be decent human beings. Some days I'm in for the fight, but to have to always exert myself isn't fair to me or my mental health.

Discernment Diagram: Entry 9

This week we had to read seven chapters from Brainwashed by Tom Burrell, and I'm not quite sure how I feel. On one hand Burrell makes a lot of valid points that I hadn't thought in-depth about from the point of view he takes up. On the other hand, though, Burrell seems to be blaming Black people for their own conditions under white supremacy, which I don't think is fair. He also states, when talking about the general inability to build strong family units, that Black women are too strong and therefore emasculating toward Black men and that this is one of the main roots of the issue. I didn't particularly appreciate that statement.

Burrell didn't talk about why Black women are so strong, and he completely ignores the fact that matriarchy was the structure by which many African tribes operated before they were captured and enslaved. A lot of Black women are strong because they have to be, and because it's an important cultural aspect of Black family life. Black women are double oppressed, underpaid, disrespected and disregarded, and often left to fend for ourselves when it comes to both growing up and raising children. Black women don't have the time to be docile and "sweet" just so men, Black or white, won't feel threatened or intimidated. Maybe instead of condemning Black women for surviving in a world meant to tear us down, Burrell should address the fragile masculinity of Black men and their dependency upon oppressive patriarchal norms as the reason for unstable Black family units. In general, it's Black men that run from the responsibility of their families, not Black women. And when the Black men who run from their families are asked why, they usually respond with statements of inadequacy and fragility. I found it odd, then, that Burrell places the blame with Black women and not Black men. As a Black woman I'm wrong for refusing to let my mind be broken by white supremacy and the Black man's internalized weakness and inferiority that results from such, but the Black man gets to keep being weak and running away and it's still all my fault? That's cute. Black women get to pick up the slack and overcompensate for their men's absences, but we don't get acknowledged for that. Instead, we get demonized for it.

Burrell makes a lot of points that I liked, though, like when he talked about Black and beautiful not having to be contradictions. I love that Black women are learning to embrace their beauty, because it's been attacked for so long. I like to say sometimes that I see queens every day, they just don't know it. But now the queens are learning that they're queens, and it's amazing to witness the change this is bringing about. We're finally discovering and embracing our Black girl magic, and it feels good. The

181

chapter "Uglified", especially when Burrell addresses Black hair, made me think about this David Banner interview that I saw this summer. Banner said that the reason Black hair has been under such scrutinized attack for so long, is because our hair grows toward God of away from Him (or Her). I'll always remember this. Black people are not superior to anyone, but we are not inferior either. I think about that in the morning when I unbraid my hair, freeing it to salute the sun that nourishes this earth. It's beautiful, because that's what Black is. They can shackle me down, try to keep me ignorant, and try to teach me to hate what nature gifted me with, but I will always rise. My mind will be free and my hair will continue to defy gravity. So far as what this means for my purpose, I'm not sure. For now I'll declare that I want to teach young people that look like me, especially young Black women, to still love themselves even if this world doesn't. I want to make it clear that it's okay to be strong and self-sufficient, and that this doesn't need to be watered down to fit into the constraints of fragile masculinity.

Discernment Diagram: Entry 10

For one of the articles for my final project I wrote a letter to anyone who wants to be free from the perils that this system has imposed upon us, and I think it aligns fairly well with what I feel my purpose to be. I'm not exactly sure what I want to be yet, as far as my career is concerned, but I do think I know what I want to say. I could do it through psychological counseling, teaching, or maybe even policy reform, but I want to deliver the message to Black people that things are not okay, change needs to occur, and that they can do it. I want them to know that it's not going to be easy, and that it's okay to get tired sometimes, and that it's okay to talk about that in a space that feels safe to them because other people get it too. We were tired, and we are tired, and the key is to stay tired because that's what happens when your eyes are always open. I want people to know that it's discouraging sometimes but it's not impossible because we, just like everyone else, deserve to have space under the sun that's not restricted by the confines of "the system" and the mentality that often times results from it.

Anyhow, here's what I wrote:

A Message to Those Who Long for Liberation

I must first start out by saying that you possess strength beyond what you dare even imagine, for this expedition is not for the faint of heart. It is crucial, then, that you understand the reasons for your oppression. They will try keep you down not for fear of your inadequacy, but for fear of your immeasurable power. It is this innate, unbeknownst power that you must grasp onto as you embark on the quest that lies in front of you, for the journey that you will travel in pursuit of mental liberation is a lonely, ill-equipped one.

No one nor anything can prepare you for the agonies and disruption that accompany such a feat, just as nothing can prepare you for the unwavering joy and ever-present inner peace that you will one day come to know. As you sit in this space reading these pages, be aware of your surroundings. You are at a highly accredited university, soon to begin a four-year journey of personal, professional, academic, and spiritual growth that will likely cause more pain than it ever will pleasure. With this, I must say to you, dear reader: be not afraid, for this is exactly where you are meant to be.

Imagine, if you will, that you are a rose awaiting its overdue bloom. As you embark on the journey towards mental liberation from the oppression systematically imposed upon your psyche, your eyes will open and learn to see what our societal captors have tried desperately to keep hidden. This knowledge will serve to be your sunlight, and your mind will serve to be your rose awaiting its unapologetic blossom. Although it will often times be uncomfortable, do not shy away from the knowledge offered to you along this voyage to true psychological freedom. It is your knowledge that will free you, and your ignorance that will keep you enslaved. Please, I beg, do not choose the comfort of the latter.

There are multiple obstacles that you will surely endure, through which you must have faith in the ultimate value of your own liberation, despite the illusory lies that have been fed to you all along. As was stated before, you will likely travel alone. Those who are enslaved around you may be too afraid to join you on your path, or they may simply be too blinded by the illusion of their freedom to recognize their continued enslavement. You will be viewed with suspicion of your sanity due solely to the fact that you desire to be anything other than a well-kept slave who enjoys only slave-like privileges. Learn to embrace this "insanity", because as the fearless revolutionary Assata Shakur once said, "Only the strong go crazy. The weak just go along." Because of this, you will likely face isolation and therefore the possible accompanied feelings of intense vulnerability, which may result in the temptation to regress back to the familiar state of your psychological enslavement. It is in times like these that you must be comfortable to trust that what you know is correct.

The process by which mental liberation is achieved is by no means an easy one. It will require wisdom, courage, and most importantly patience for our fellow Black people. The enslavement to which you are subjected is not your fault, and you, just as they, have been encouraged to blindly settle for the mere illusion of freedom without the true implementation of such. It will be disheartening to gain awareness of the problematic nature of many African-American norms that we so desperately want to believe are okay. It will be tumultuous, painful, and ultimately exhausting, but it is NOT more than you can handle. At times you may be tempted to surrender, but you must remain conscious of the lives sacrificed not for the mere illusion of your freedom, but rather for the just reality of it.

Finally, while you are on this journey, I ask you to please remember this: just as a flower deserves to bloom, you deserve to know freedom, truly and unapologetically.

Stay woke,
Sequoia Patterson-Johnson

***

Since taking EDXC242, Anti-Black Racism and Epistemic Violence, I have begun to develop a critical lens through which I analyze the intellectual spaces I occupy, and which I cannot ever take off. With the knowledge offered to me in EDXC242 I am now able to more accurately identify the tools of oppression employed against me. Since taking this class, I can't help but critically analyze every piece of knowledge taught to me as if it is truth, because I have been taught to look beyond face value and define truth for myself.

This has become exceedingly crucial, as I am currently undergoing the long, tedious, and often times grueling process of earning a Bachelor of Science in Psychology. Before EDCX242 I accepted the information presented to me in classrooms to be truth, even though such information blatantly excludes people of color. I remember genuinely thinking, and blindly trusting, that what costs more than $50,000 a year to learn was all that was there to know about the field of psychology. Because of this, I also remember feeling very displaced, lost, and alienated, as if my sense of purpose had no place in the world that I was being "prepared" for. At the great white institution from which I am receiving my education, I learn solely about psychological theory developed by dead, rich white men, read about psychological studies conducted on middle and upper middle class white people, and receive instruction from white professors who routinely mispronounce my first name, as if its spelling is not phonetic. In my four years of college education in my major's department, I have never even had a professor who looks like me, and in my time here I have certainly not learned about the psychology of anyone who looks like me.

My intellectual experiences, now, are shaped by the realization that I pay tuition just to be deprived of knowledge pertinent to my lived experiences. I pinch pennies together to afford the deprivation of knowledge, which I need in order to make sense of myself and the ways in which I have reacted to the stifling anti-Blackness that plagues my existence. My intellectual experiences are shaped, largely, by my feelings of deeply rooted anger, betrayal, and heartbreaking disappointment.

The Book of Sequoia

When we don't talk about the Black experience in fields like psychology, we function only to fail to our prepare students, the future psychologists of this world, to effectively mend the psyches of Black people whose psyches have formed under conditions of duress, fear, and indoctrinated inferiority since before their frontal lobes could even form long-term memories. When we strategically avoid the study and discussion of the Black experience in America, and every other colonized land in this world we claim to be ours, we exclude those same Black people from adequate psychological care. We instead, by way of such exclusion, continue to produce culturally incompetent psychologists, counselors, social workers, and psychiatrists, who know only how to operate from the foundation of an education centered around the lie of whiteness repeatedly shoved down every one of our throats. By performing such depriving acts of violence over the knowledge available to young, hungry minds, we

188

inherently promise that Black people will continue to be alienated and marginalized from the psychological care we attempt to seek, most often to help us cope with the psychological traumas that result from lifelong alienation, marginalization, and systemic victimization.

As I sit through my classes, this is what I think about. When I took Abnormal Psychology last semester, and I learned about the various depressive and anxiety disorders that plague every one in five American people. While in this, I was disappointed in my professor because he seemed not to know to tell the class that Black Americans experience depression and anxiety at nearly twice the rate than our white counterparts. That same professor also seemed not to know to inform the class about how such depression and anxiety stems from the weight of Black people, who from age five or earlier, must routinely embody various masks of whiteness to survive in a white world. In that class, we didn't learn about how painful, or how psychologically damaging, it is to swallow, hide, and try to exterminate one's Blackness and the various aspects of one's identity marked by such Blackness, for a narrow mold of whiteness into which we will never be able to fit. We also never learned about how psychologically damaging it is for Black people to be told, through people's abrasive and fearful reactions to our mere existence, that we are inherently problematic in all that we do, when we long to be perceived as normal, and to feel like we belong.

Because I am aware of the epistemologically violent acts committed against me in predominantly white intellectual spaces, I constantly find myself choosing between fighting the battle of attempting to educate my sometimes stubbornly-ignorant educators and the internal battle of remaining silent so that I may get through class without fighting a fight for which I do not have the energy. In many of my undergraduate intellectual experiences after EDXC242, I have been the silently angry Black woman in the front row of class (and never the back, because God forbid I give people yet another superficial reason to doubt my intellectual ability) because I simply do not want to be the vocally angry Black woman, frequently expending my precious energy debating with professors of mine who have never learned to even consider the relative validity of the truth I dare to propose to them. While I take notes, discuss theories, and write papers, I grapple tirelessly with the notion that my enlightenment and education may not ever, at least in my undergraduate career, occur in the same spaces despite the fact that they both depend so heavily on one another.

Part III: Door of Know Return

I know my parents love me,
Stand behind me come what may.
I know now that I'm ready,
Because I finally heard them say,
It's a different world from where you come from.
Here's a chance to make it,
If we focus on our goals.
If you dish it, we can take it,
Just remember you've been told.
It's a different world from where you come from.
It's a different world from where you come from.
- Stu Gardner, Bill Cosby and Dawnn Lewis

Chapter 9: Bone, Blood, and Harmony

My dissertation is the first published work in which I deeply engage anti-Black racism and epistemic violence. I watched an episode of the television sitcom A Different World each day as I wrote it. This show first aired September 24, 1987, the same year and two months before I was born. I felt there was a divine connection between its contents and the context of my life. A Different World told stories that I needed to hear in order to sustain the journey I was on as an emerging Black intellectual. I believe that the stories we pass along can serve as intergenerational medicine that heals the wounds of social ills internally and externally. These narratives have the power to generate the kind of knowing that helps us recover and return to a place of being centered. In the preface of this book, I tell the story behind the artwork on the cover. It is an artistic recreation of a photo from my first trip to Senegal, West

Blood, Bone, and Harmony

Africa. While I was in country, I visited the House of Slaves on Gorée Island. On the evening after visiting Gorée I wrote:

They call it the "door of no return," but today I returned. I walked in with all of my Detroit. I walked in with all of the 1800s, 1900s, and recent trauma of Black people in America. I returned. The tears began the moment I walked in the "House." I did not need to see the rooms. I knew them. My spirit knew where I was. My bones remembered. Like Legos, I fell in place. Brick block by brick block, my hands touched the rooms of every passage. I felt unbearable sorrow. Pain in my blood came running from my eyes and down my cheeks like bitter tea. I knew the history but today, it was as if I was hearing it for the first time.

That day, I learned that Gorée means dignity. It is one of the most painfully beautiful places I have ever seen. Learning the meaning of the word in contrast to the meaning left behind because of the Trans-Atlantic Slave Trade, I was deeply reminded of the ways that epistemic violence can redefine what was glorious as something to be mourned. There is an art installation at the African Renaissance Monument there in Senegal that illustrates this "Door of No Return" between the body and words of Dr. Martin Luther King, Jr. and the body and words Barack Obama. The words read, "I have a dream…Yes we can," and there is an enslaved African between them sitting at "The Door of No Return." This visual has stayed with me since. I think of the door in the art display as the Door of Know Return. To know something is to be aware of it. To return is to come back after a period of physical absence, or to turn your attention back to something after a period of time. The door of know return is the opportunity to draw one's attention back to the observations and information that can lead to new pathways. It is going back to the entrance of an enclosed space and retrieving what you need to resolve the uncertainty about where you can go. It is an invitation to Sankofa. It is finding your way back through the door of no return. The door of know return is a passage towards and back to "a different world from where you come from." For some students, this door may be purely metaphorical. For others, it is real and tangible. No matter how you come to it, the challenge is to walk through it.

What was profound to me about my experience on Gorée was the remembering in my blood and bones. Researchers have documented that memories can be passed down through DNA and other African Americans have written about having similar experiences to mine. Nevertheless, the physical realization of this truth made me genuinely feel part of something greater. The interconnections that I understood but could not explain validated my belongingness in the diasporic community. It also intensified a yearning I had to situate and validate the different way of knowing that I was a carrier of. The first two sections of this book deal heavily with the concept of self and with one's ability to leverage self-awareness as intellectual activism. The Door of Know Return is about communal agency and reclamation. It is about relationship and the sacred healing that exists between those who are of the same blood and bone. The final question I posed in the introduction of this book was: How can a classroom become a space of reconciliation and healing for students who are trying to dismantle anti-Black racism while living in an era where violence against Black bodies, Black minds, and Black futures is on the rise? The response to this question can be generated by examining the relationship between blood, bone, and harmony. Let's begin...

***

When I returned from Senegal I traveled to Washington D.C. for an annual student leadership experience. While there, I was in a conversation with Dr.

199

Blood, Bone, and Harmony

Debyii Sababu-Thomas and she said to me, "The wiser you become, the more you will realize that 1+1=3." We were discussing the topic of marriage and she was making a point that a healthy marriage includes the person you are, the person your spouse is, and what you two become together. No person, she said, should lose or sacrifice themselves for the sake of the whole because the whole can only exist when there are two different parts to bring it together. What she was describing was a kind of harmony, if you will, that is possible to build in human relationships.

The word harmony seems like a simple term and most would assume that everyone shares the same definition. So when students, for example, say they want more "harmony" and peace on their campuses, they think everyone envisions the same outcome. Marimba Ani (1994) points out that the idea of harmony actually has contradicting meanings in Western/Eurocentric theories and in Eastern and Afrocentric theories. Ani writes that in the Eurocentric worldview harmony is "…projected as rational order, an order based on the mechanism of control."xi She informs us that, "What Plato recognizes as "harmony" [for example] is achieved when the "positive" term of the dichotomy controls (or destroys) the "negative" term/phenomenon/entity: when reason controls emotion both in person and in the state."xii According to Ani, non-Eurocentric perspectives of harmony are achieved through the balancing of pairs. Harmony therefore, is not about the control of one entity over the other, but instead is created when complementary forces interact without destroying each other (1+1=3). Simply put, Eurocentric harmony means that the "good" should have control over the "bad." When put in these terms, many students struggle with finding a reason not to agree, but, when what is considered "good" is male, white, cis-gender, or wealthy, it should become much easier to see why this version of harmony is dangerous.

Blood, Bone, and Harmony

Under a Platonic conception of harmony, the notion of peace can only exist when the best control the worst; the strong control the weak, the rational control the emotional. If such "balance" gets out of hand, there can be no "peace." We see examples of this kind of thinking all over social media, and many of us have thought this way ourselves, as most of us have been educated under Eurocentric curricula. We do not see a reason why what we consider "good" should not control the "bad," so therefore, we spend most of time debating what the "good" is and demanding that our definition of "good" have its turn at controlling the "bad." This influences how authority, punishment, truth, and freedom are experienced in schools. Plato believed that the hard work of attaining this kind of control could only be achieved by a small number of people, thus giving way to the logical reason why the few should rule over many. Under this way of thinking, this epistemology, one entity

Blood, Bone, and Harmony

must mute and dominate the other because peace is established by taking control.

Most students are familiar with Plato and his writings, but will likely not be familiar with any Eastern or Afrocentric theorists who proposed a different way of being in the world. Therefore, what they will draw on, what shapes their thinking, is often one sided and constantly recycled, thus perpetuating the belief that it works. So when students at a rally say "No justice, no peace" they are not thinking that their words could be reinforcing the very oppression they are trying to dismantle. I've had students ask me if the point of the struggle to end anti-Black racism was just so that Black people could then control White people. They had no ability to imagine a world where one group of people did not control or oppress another. I am also aware that the fear of such a takeover keeps many who benefit from the current state of affairs from considering change, even as chaos and despair thickens. This lack of ability to consider a different way of thinking, is another example of the harm done by epistemic violence. But, what about Eastern and Afrocentric versions of harmony? How can they be achieved on our campuses? Or should they? Could they be just as epistemically violent toward us?

As I considered my responses to these questions, I began to think of what harmony looks like in some religious worlds. I recalled an article I read once about the 1+1=3 concept that Dr. Sababu-Thomas mentioned. The article was written by a Jewish Rabbixiii who argued that the number one represents something that exists alone. Unity in this sense is solitude and peace that comes from not being disturbed. The Rabbi described the number two as a metaphor for complexity and duality. Two represented tension and discord. Finally, the number three was defined as a symbol of harmony that results from a union. Three did not emerge because the number two destroyed one, leaving one left to return to its place of solitude and peace.

Blood, Bone, and Harmony

Contrastingly, the number three symbolized harmony because it merged one and two together in a way that created a new entity where opposites could exist together. The Rabbi puts this in the context of the way that Jews (and Christians) believe the world was created. According to Jewish and Christian texts, it was on the third day that God made it possible for air and water, light and dark, land and sea to work together and called that day and every day after "good." Day two was not referred to as a "good" day; it was when separation had taken place. On day one no other life existed but God, in solitude and unity with God only.

Perhaps there is divine irony in leveraging support for Eastern and Afrocentric versions of harmony in the bible. Nevertheless, Afrocentric notions of harmony are repeatedly expressed as ways to address the state of affairs in this country. In The Healing Wisdom of Africaxiv, Malidoma Patrice Somé writes that the Western and Afrocentric worlds can coexist and promote understanding between one another that would serve to heal the ills within them both. He describes them both as part of one whole, which if by nothing else, are united by the fact they have both chosen to exist on the earth. I do not think the notion of coexisting is a new concept for college students. Many of you have access to the global world through technology that makes it easier to conceive of such a place. But in a country that professes itself to be a place where we secure the blessing of liberty to ourselves and our posterity, we must own the lack of credibility for being able to exist without destroying our chosen "other."

I think that it is important that college students of any background take the time to wrestle with words we take for granted, like harmony and peace, and trace their understanding to the roots that give it definition. I often ask students, "How do you know that?" Their response sometimes is, "I don't know, I just do." Without even second-guessing, they have come to "know" many things without knowing how or why. This generation has experienced a teach to the test culture that leaves very little time in any teacher's schedule for critical academic exploration or the questioning of how and why we know what we know. Epistemic violence, therefore, is somewhat of a silent eradicator. It is far rarer that we are asked to identify the lessons in our minds that teach us to be, think, and see anti-Black racism as normal and inevitable, even if we consider ourselves to be anti-racist.

Envisioning what peace and harmony looks like from multiple perspectives opens the door for students to begin to imagine what racial justice looks like. I want to posit in your thinking that such efforts only find meaning as one seeks and deepens their sense of community. The tedious and painful process of discovering and dismantling anti-black racism and epistemic violence is all for naught if it does not lead to deeper experiences of love and relationship in community. As one begins to build their cultural competence, they will recognize that different cultures have varying perspectives on how to exist in community; some preferring individualism to collectivism. This difference provides lived tensions for people of the African Diaspora, as the memories in our blood and bones are not always in harmony with the cultures that have colonized us. Thus, creating spaces of healing and reconciliation for such students cannot be simply about the spaces we share with others but the space that exists between ourselves. As mentioned previously, anti-racist efforts often focus on the relationship between groups and not within. Repairing the gashes of epistemic violence and anti-Black racism necessitate that Black students have space to engage and experience their diasporic community. I would argue that all groups need such a space but want to emphasize the necessity for Black students because much of their ability to generate Black intellectualism is stifled by the fact that they cannot connect with the sources of indigenous power that generate it. Therefore, it becomes imperative that they be challenged and supported in doing more than addressing anti-black racism as it pertains to whiteness and white supremacy. A classroom becomes a site for such healing when it serves as an incubator for Black knowledge production and permits a bridging of intellectual worlds that are at odds. Harmony for diasporic souls cannot require the dominance or destruction of one over the other, as we are the intersections of both. Our histories, our ancestors, and thus our epistemologies are intertwined and interdependent. The amalgamation is perhaps where our greatest sense of community and perhaps the deepest level of healing can be achieved.

Reclamation of a Colonized World

Chapter 10: Reclamation of the Colonized world

The Cost of Dead Dreams

My soul looks out and wonders, what happened to my
Dream. Like a mother, awaiting the return of her child
home, my longing is bursting at the seam. I wait with
expecting urgency, just to see his face again, I've never
been able to shake the memory of the cage they put him in.
He got lost in the tangled reality of *US* and Justice.
Someone took hold of him and held him captive until a
ransom was paid to set him free, but he was bought in...
blood. Blood. The most controversial commodity, draped in
detached philosophies, backed by unfulfilled prophecies
and my soul cannot find its Dream! Every day I staple
"Missing" signs on neighborhood trees with the question
that reads, "Have you seen my dream? My soul holds
rallies, calls in a search team, and just like the events
described in the movie Changeling[1], the community tries to
convince my soul that its dream has been found. They have
given me an imposter! They tell me that I am crazy,
delusional not to recognize my own Dream. But I know it is
not him.

My soul looks out and wonders, if the Dream will ever
come home. If he has grown, will he look different, will he
recognize me? In August of 1963, a young man spotted my
dream on the steps of the Lincoln Memorial! He told the
story of where my Dream had been and how a man named
Abraham Lincoln had found my dream 5 score years ago,
adopted him and renamed him Emancipation Proclamation.

Reclamation of a Colonized World

My Dream had been seared in the flames of withering injustice but this man, *Martin*, had seen him and he knew where he was. I rejoiced at the thought of my Dream returning to me!

My soul had waited so long! It was 240 years ago when I let my Dream visit a governor in Virginia. I had wanted him to run free. To manifest the life, liberty, and pursuit of happiness I put inside him. See, my Dream had been desired by many! He was so bright, vivid like LED lights. Tens of millions from all nations came to see him dance on the shores. He had the ability to convince then to study war no more, to work hard, and not settle for being "poor." Unrestricted by barriers, folks saw him and knew they would no longer be carriers,
of social orders developed to benefit one person at the expense of another. After all, I was his mother! I taught him to open doors.

I waited for the day my Dream would return home to me. So when I finally heard a knock on my door, I rose from my chair, readied my soul, and answered the door with expecting urgency! "Ms. America?" the officer said, "may we come in?" I ushered them into my living room and held the door open a little longer, hoping my dream would walk in behind them.
I did not see him. Perhaps he was waiting in the car. I took a seat and waited for the announcement of our reunion. But that was not what they had come to tell me. America, your dream is dead, they told me.

In fact, he had never been carried to full term. I had not birthed him. He was dead inside of me, and the presence of his decayed reality had made me sick. Like a pregnant mother overdue, my soul had grown tired and anxious trying to induce contractions and force the birth of a nation conceived hundreds of years ago. Stunned by their words, I felt like the world had stood still. I heard the tick tock of the clock on my wall, smelled the burning wood in my fireplace, the room felt like it was closing in on me. I wanted to run. The officer began to tell me about all the researchers who had been working my case, how they discovered my dead dream, and the cause of his death. Instantly, I felt as if I hand nothing left, as they told me it was a virus that had killed my beloved dream.

Infected in utero, my Dream had nowhere to go, when the virus came on the scene. I could barely hear their voices over the sound of my pain, when a man asked if I was still with them. That's when I heard them say it was a virus called *racism*. Instantly, I fell to my knees in tears and said it could not be true! My Dream lives! Just then, a woman named Assata, touched me on my shoulder and said she was sorry for my loss. She said many had paid the cost in search of the American dream. That it was our duty to fight for his freedom, but the fight wasn't what it seemed. She reminded me of the many names we gave him, the bold people who had given their lives to save him, and the Captors who tried to lay claim to him! They told me it was time I had surgery to have the dead dream removed from my body.

I felt numb. My dream had been perfect. How could I let them take it away from me?

This dis-ease, this racism, they said claimed the life of my dream, it can't be what it seems- But if it is, racism is what they should be out looking for. How dare they come to my door, without finding a cure for what was killing me softly as I speak, I grow weak at the sheer thought that anything they said could be true. See I had clothed my baby in red, white and blue. My beloved dream. I was enraged! Just as I turned to walk away, a man in a black hat asked me….

What happens to a dream deferred[xv]?
 Does it dry up
 like a raisin in the sun?
 Or fester like a sore—
 And then run?
 Does it stink like rotten meat?
 Or crust and sugar over—
 like a syrupy sweet?
 Maybe it just sags
 like a heavy load.
 Or does it explode?

Reclamation of a Colonized World

This chapter begins with a modified version of a talk I delivered for TEDx Xavier in 2016. It is a story I told about America, through the eyes of a mother (Ms. America) who believed her child (the American Dream) was missing only to discover that she was delusional and that the remains of her unborn child were still in her womb. I named racism as being the virus that had attacked the dream in her womb. The woman in the poem represents the perspective of an individual who will not accept the reality of the infectious nature of racism because of the pain it would cause and because admitting the death of the "dream" would be to give up on its life and all the promising things that came along with it. Confronting racism can feel this way, particularly since the American Dream is espoused as something anyone can achieve. Drawing attention to the flaws within the birth of this country can make people angry, cause them to lash out, and shut down. The poem ends with questions from Langston

Reclamation of a Colonized World

Hughes' poem, A Dream Deferred. I offered these questions as an opportunity for reflection about what happens when dreams die. What happened to the dream of America when it was not fully realized? If we admit that it is not possible to buy freedom with slavery, independence with dependency, and rights with wrongdoings, how do we reconcile the past? If we acknowledge the deep presence of epistemic violence in our colleges and universities, will racism sag like a heavy load, or does it explode? I posed these questions to the students in my classroom. Many of them referenced recent tragedies as the explosions. We began to reflect on what it will take to heal ourselves, our communities, and our nation. In this process, I asked, "Can we reclaim a colonized culture?" Here is what they had to say…

Reclamation of a Colonized World

TZ:

There are measures of forgiveness which one must learn to wrestle with before, and most certainly after, raising the question of reclaiming a colonized culture. This is because one cannot believe that it is possible to reclaim anything colonized if one cannot endure to reclaim their own being. I think that there are so many things we wish not to see in ourselves. To begin to see ourselves, we must know how to forgive ourselves, perpetually, for what we find. I do not believe it is my position to tell you, dear reader, how you must learn to forgive yourself. It is your forgiveness that remains for discovery. I would be beyond my own integrity if I suggested that I know how to forgive myself, though I know I must. Nor do I wish to, with immediacy at least, encourage you toward some Holy

217

Book, as the problem of colonization does not disappear when questions of scripture, authorship and the color of God are raised. What I am certain of, if I am to be certain of anything, is that the project of forgiveness requires love, and love requires a will to love, a tolerance for believing beyond that which the world defines as lovable, and a willingness to explore that which different communities define as being worthy of love.

I am not certain that colonized peoples have the outright desire to forgive colonizers; I am even less certain that there is love in this relationship – besides, of course, the love that remains in spite of tragedy. Yet, even in observance of the fact that colonized people go on about their lives without erupting each day into a civil war demanding reparation and reconciliation, I am drawn to observe the moral fortitude of colonized cultures, especially Black cultures. Perhaps the collective body of the Diaspora is Christ incarnate. Perhaps we are not as empty as our colonizers wish us to believe we are. Perhaps there is something living and breathing in the Black body, which has an insurmountable will to survive. Perhaps the allure of this natural resource has fed the insatiable desperation of colonizers.

In any case, time knows no reversals. Reclaiming colonized culture is imagining an uncolonized future. Accepting the challenge of imagination, however, is no fairytale. We are asking of ourselves, in a sense, to be all that we've never been. And, to be all that we've never been, we must know, completely, all that we are. Despite the presumed impossibility of our efforts, we must always believe it is possible. By doing so, we will see clearly our power and, hopefully, stand firm in the aftermath of our devastation. Above all, we must accept the impossibility of our efforts all the while observing that our Freedom Dreams[xvi] are, in fact, coming true. I suppose the idea of liberation lies at the intersection of this paradox: impossible and happening. Furthermore, I believe this paradox carries within it a time paradox. We needn't be any less of ourselves today than we were yesterday. There is freedom behind forgiveness and we need time and patience to unearth ourselves. The lesson of reclaiming asserts, therefore, that we must not rush, but, we certainly cannot wait.

Reclamation of a Colonized World

EO:

In Ousmane Sembene's first feature film, *Black Girl* (1966)[xvii], the main character, Diouana, is hired as a maid by a white French family residing in Dakar, Senegal. On her first day of work, she gifts her employers a traditional mask she bought from a little boy as a token of her gratitude to them for hiring her. Diouana relocates to France to continue to work for the family only to learn that she is treated like a slave. Frustrated by the way she is being treated, Diouana begins to resent her employers. When she has had enough, she takes the mask that is hanging on a wall and packs her bag. The madam realizes the mask is gone and finds it in Diouana's room and tries to take it from her. She and Diouana then struggle for the mask, Diouana insisting that the mask belongs to her. This scene in *Black Girl* is where my mind is drawn when I imagine the process of reclaiming a colonized culture.

Reclamation of a Colonized World

In my mind, the first step is the colonized realizing that they are not being helped or aided by the presence of colonization. In the movie, Diouana initially operates with the mindset that her employers are helping her and, in buying the mask from the boy and giving it to them, becomes complicit in her own colonization. It is not until Diouana realizes that her employers do not care about her wellbeing that she rebels. In *Yurugu: An Afrikan-Centered Critique of European Cultural Thought and Behavior*[xviii], Marimba Ani writes, "the costly political error of non-European converts has been to think that they would ever be included in the European 'Christian brotherhood' in the same way they were part of their own cultures." It is in the realization that the culture in which we function is not to our benefit that we can begin to reclaim and construct one that does.

The second step is rooted in an understanding that "culture doesn't make people, people make culture.[xix]" We have the power to define our culture the way we want to; to question traditions that ostracize and eradicate practices that do not align with who we know ourselves to be in the current age. Defining who we are, not relative to anyone else but by and for ourselves, on our own terms will allow us take back what was colonized. The reclamation must be in service to only ourselves. Concentrating on proving ourselves to the colonizers or educating them is "an old and primary tool of all oppressors to keep the oppressed occupied with the master's concerns.[xx]"

This process, however, may not result in full reclamation. In the process of colonization, there is destruction and eradication of elements that can never be recovered. A part of reclamation needs to be redefinition and re-imagination. An example of this is the re-imagination of the character M'Baku for the movie *Black Panther* (2018)[xxi]. In the comics, M'Baku was known as "Man-Ape," a depiction that was racist and rooted in the

223

colonial perception of Africans. Director, Ryan Coogler, was able to reimagine the character in a way that celebrated M'Baku's connection to nature rather than demonizing it. In reclaiming colonized cultures, there also needs to be an effort to remember what was stolen and re-member the pieces that were torn apart. Reclamation of a colonized culture is more about the process of reclaiming and the restorative healing that comes with it.

Reclamation of a Colonized World

DB:

I believe that we have the ability to reclaim culture(s) that has been colonized. While we may not have the ability to restore it to its original state I believe we can still take it and mold it into something new. In many ways I feel that this is exactly what's been done with Black Culture in America. Overcoming epistemic violence feels to me like a far more difficult task to tackle. I don't believe it is impossible to overcome however I will say that it would have to be done in a very strategic way, one that would take time to even begin to formulate. Just as racism is ingrained in our society I feel that EV being a product of racism is also ingrained in the very foundation of this country. Due to this we'd have to essentially deconstruct and reconstruct this nation, at least to some degree, to complete such a task. Similar to reclaiming culture I think restoring knowledge is possible and even in a way currently happening. I think a large part of restoring knowledge is

Reclamation of a Colonized World

making history of all cultures part of curriculum as opposed to white Eurocentric history. I also believe reading and studying different texts from different places is a way of restoring knowledge as you get a full picture of a story as opposed to one side, generally the side of the oppressors or victors that we usually receive.

Reclamation of a Colonized World

AP:

The question to me is not whether we can reclaim a
colonized culture but whether we *want* to reclaim a
colonized culture? This thought comes from the idea that
we cannot change the fact that we have interacted with the
European and in that interaction we have been affected in
ways that we would not have been had we not. African-
Americans specifically have been ripped from our
homeland and our culture ripped from us for the sake of
survival. I hold the belief, in agreement with James
Baldwin, that we cannot deny the fact that African-
Americans and white people are connected by blood. With
that in mind, it makes the black experience all the more
unique and complex. We have a culture that we have both
made and had forced on us and in trying to reclaim our
African heritage we must be mindful that we do not attempt
to become what we are not. At this point we are a different
people that will always be connected to both the continent

227

Reclamation of a Colonized World

and Africa and the United States as a country and because of this we are our own. As much as I want to be able to reclaim my culture that was stolen from me, I wonder how much of me will still feel out of place because the white culture was taught to me for so long and even now as I attempt to gain Afro-centric knowledge, epistemic violence still limits my ability to conceptualize new arguments and ideas. But that is not all bad because in the ability to reclaim the old we are able to create a new.

My biggest issue with theology is that as a study that affects the moral compass of so many, it focuses too much on the past and not enough on the future. By trying to reclaim a colonized culture, I fear that we may fall into the same pattern of focusing too much on the past and not enough on the future. What African-Americans believe to be the colonized culture may be and probably is different from what Africans believe used to be the culture. That disconnect to me is not all bad, in fact I think it is critical in

228

our ability to come together using both perspectives. In creating a new we may come to discover that our inherent spirits led us back to the old. I believe that even in that case however, it is not a reclaiming as much as it is a rediscovery process.

Reclamation of a Colonized World

SPJ:

I write to you today in the language of my ancestors' captors, enslavers, rapists, and psychological tormenters. When I speak in this foreign English tongue, the only one that I know how to use, the tone in my voice embodies the unimaginable scrutiny that has plagued my lineage for centuries after their royalty and dignity was stolen from them. I am not English, but English is what I know. So, as I attempt to answer this complex question, of whether or not a colonized culture can be reclaimed, I felt that I must first answer with this, because I am only capable of expressing my intellectual capacity through a language that should not be mine. My tongue, my expression, the tangible vocalization of everything my soul feels, is merely a product of many lifetimes of colonization, deprivation, and theft. That being said, I do not know if I can ever reclaim a culture that has been stolen from the melanated

Reclamation of a Colonized World

people whose brilliant bright red blood courses tirelessly through my veins.

If I am to ponder whether or not a colonized culture can be reclaimed, I must first ask what my culture is. What is our culture? I know not what parts of Africa my ancestors' blue-black bodies were stolen from, or the tribes from which my Native American forerunners came. I do not know the languages they spoke, the hairstyles that were uniquely theirs, or the ways in which they channeled the deep spirituality that lie within each one of them, far too great to be suppressed. I have, as a result, only known the horrid sense of loss, despair, brokenness, and confusion that comes from me not knowing who my ancestors were, and therefore the fullness of who I am. Be this as it may, it makes more sense to answer whether or not I can heal from the brokenness that colonization has made mine.

In order to do so, I must do three things:

Reclamation of a Colonized World

1. Commit to discovering knowledge of African people before enslavement came to define their livelihoods. In order to reclaim my queenship, I must allow myself to know of its full power.

2. Release the fear of myself, which I have learned. I am Black, but it does not mean I am as angry, or an dangerous as "they" told me I was. I can be gentle, and intelligent, and passionate, without demonizing the results of my own growth.

3. Blossom, freely and unapologetically. My mind and the essence of my spirit are beautiful flowers just beginning to blossom. This journey of enlightenment that I am on is my sunlight, from which I will not shy away, but rather I will bask proudly, and affirmed in its warmth.

***

These reflections all carry within them distinct tensions and concerns that are indicative of the varying

232

stages of the continuum that students situate their understanding. It is less important that there is agreement or consensus as a response to the question but more important that individuals be given the space to consume and produce their own meanings. On the cover of the book, there are boats coming in, together. They are representations of the return of wholeness for all those whose lineage, customs, bodies, and hearts have been broken by the onslaught of anti-Black racism. Reclamation is just one of the boats that sail alongside recognition, restoration, reparation, and reconciliation. The Door of Know Return is an invitation to begin this journey together.

Selah

Selah: An Epilogue

The meaning of the word Selah and its origin are unknown. Throughout centuries, different people have said what they think it means, but no one person's interpretation has been accepted as the original definition of the word. Selah is written seventy-four times in the Bible, yet not even Biblical scholars can say with certainty where it comes from and what it really means. Selah, therefore, is a word that has meaning only in the context of the one you give it. Some writers use it to indicate the end of a musical line or as an indication that one should pause and reflect. For these reasons, Selah is befitting as the title of the final portion of this book. Redefining what you know and giving yourself the space to reflect in this process is a sacred necessity for overcoming epistemic violence. The three sections of the book are part of a trifold strategy for how to see and then respond to anti-Black racism and epistemic violence in fresh ways that should include a Selah. Your Selah is the opportunity for you to become fully aware of your creative transcendence. It is the space that you generate and use to ruminate on what you have brought into existence. Of the most precious constructions to ponder in your Selah is the fully actualized self. Knowing who you are, makes who you are, worthy knowing. What you think and what you do have the potential to shift paradigms. However, such a shift requires the healing and emergence of new relationships between different epistemologies. To foster this shifting, you will have to give new meaning to existing paradigms and actively redeem yourself and your ways of knowing. Redeem as in compensate for the faults of the cultures you inhabit and redeem as in regain possession over epistemologies that have been stolen from you. Finally, you must orient your techniques to sustain the innovation you bring into the world around building and being in community. The tedious and painful process of discovering and dismantling anti-black racism and epistemic violence is all for naught if it does not lead to deeper experiences of love and relationship in community. Without community, any labor done to deconstruct anti-Blackness is a risky act of martyrdom that sacrifices the soul for the sake of the system. Therefore, community and your relationship within it is the anchor you must find and hold on to.

You will notice that Part I begins with me describing my interactions with another scholar, an elder scholar and now ancestor. I believe wholeheartedly that knowledge is communal, and that the opportunities we have for exchange with our elders can be life-giving, life-sustaining, and life-changing. This portion of the book was titled the Birth of Django Praxis because it focuses on the scaffolding that is necessary for the creation of new foundations that will withstand the onslaught of epistemic violence. Part one is not intended to tell you what to think, but to invite you to consider new notions on *how* to think. Retooling our minds on how we think about ourselves individually and how we think about the world around us is strenuous. What is important to accompany the work described in part one is the intentionality towards self-care it requires. Understanding anti-Black racism and unpacking its role and existence in your life is not abstract. It is deeply personal and labor intensive. Part two contains redemption psalms that demonstrate the trajectory of this labor-intensive process. It is intended to remind the reader of the internal medicine that we generate in our personal narratives; the organic antibiotics for resisting epistemicide. Finally, part three invites the reader to consider where one can go on the journey to dismantle anti-Black racism and epistemic violence. What does reclamation and reconciliation look like? Where must we begin repair in order to sustain reclamation and reconciliation? The concept of the door of know return is an invitation to begin the epistemological repairs in community that should accompany ontological and economic reparations. This work finds its meaning and becomes truly transformative when it is aimed at achieving love and sacred relationship within community. Generating and then walking through your own door of know return is crucial to your healing, the African diaspora, and the world. As you define and experience your Selah, I caution you to remember that engaging your mind, body, and spirit in these processes is painful. Studies show that anti-Black racism has physical implications on the health of its sufferers and such implications should be considered and monitored with intention. As you embark on a journey towards a more whole world, keep your own wholeness as a priority. Here are a few simple strategies for self-care to assist you on your journey:

Selah

❖ Journaling. Sometimes our minds are easier to put to rest when our thoughts are manifested on paper.

❖ Restorative Yoga Practices. Finding physical and mental balance helps you recover from engaging social imbalances like ABR and EV.

❖ Create a Life Soundtrack. Music is healing. Generate a list of songs that bring back positive memories of your lifespan and name your playlist according to you life's purpose.

❖ Unplug. One day a week with no electronic communication or devices can drastically improve your ability to recharge your own batteries.

Selah.

Selah

"Emptiness just means we're not aware of our own credentials. Battle scars mean that we survived... You are stronger than you think you are. "- Rene Marie

- *December 9, 2017 on Flight 416 somewhere over the Atlantic Ocean*

Selah

I watched the sun rise over the ocean. Clouds lookin' like
afros; scattered about like vegetation for the masses. Crops
at sea. Seeds of ancestors past. Subdued by purple hues,
orange glaze, and the calm of blue oasis. As I rested my
head against the window I remembered God. They (re)
membered me. Mine eyes had seen the glory of the coming
of the Sun. Finally, I was returning home. As the sun
expanded, the clouds looked les like mounds of hair and
more like pillows. Maybe I was becoming more awake.
Maybe it was God showing me the resting place of the
souls of black folk. I breathed deeply and recalled the
nameless souls I was soaring with and above. I could feel
blood running warm in my body as I thought about my
ancestors that survived long enough for me to now exist.
For God knows their names, their language, their
knowledge, their truth. I came, knowing only of their
purple hues and orange glaze. The knowledge painted of
them in the country responsible for their epistemicide. I

242

Selah

pray their wisdom finds its way into my ears like the sweet

pillow talk of a deep love. I pray that wisdom flows

through this book like the unrestricted waves of the ocean...

Selah.

Featured Student Authors

Featured Student Authors

Eseoghene Obrimah

Eseoghene Obrimah is a senior Marketing major with minors in Innovation and Digital Innovation, Film and Television. She is from Lagos, Nigeria and intends to work in film and television to fulfill her purpose of telling stories that address the complexities of being African on the continent and in the diaspora.

Adrian T. Parker Jr.

Adrian T. Parker Jr. is a senior in the Philosophy, Politics, & the Public Honors Program with a theology minor. Mr. Parker is from St. Louis, MO and desires to work in Higher Education as a professor. He believes his purpose is to create a space for students to engage with authenticity and responsive education in a way that impacts

245

their thinking concerning social responsibility, love and reconciliation.

Taylor Azi Zachary

Taylor Zachary is a senior Philosophy major with a concentration in anti-colonial literature. He was born and raised in Antioch, California. Zachary is a critical analyst on the experiences of Black college athletes and has presented his research as a TEDx speaker. Upon graduation, Mr. Zachary intends to take advantage of various endeavors that allow him to be a gallant problem solver, a courageous seeker of truth and a fearless writer.

Sequoia E. Patterson-Johnson

Sequoia Patterson-Johnson is a senior majoring in Psychology with a minor in Africana Studies. Upon graduation, she will attend graduate school to become a clinical psychologist or a civil rights attorney. Sequoia believes her purpose isn't to heal, but to aid others in their own healing journey. She does not want to be a voice for others, but seeks to aid people in the discovery and reclamation of their own voices. Sequoia seeks to dismantle nobody-ness and professes that God put her here to see the "unseen" or ignored, and gifted her with percipience and a strong voice, which she will undoubtedly use in her career.

Diamond S. Brown

Diamond Brown is a senior Psychology major with minors in Deaf Studies and Gender and Diversity Studies. Diamond believes that her purpose is to use creativity as an avenue to achieve healing concerning mental health disparities in Black communities. Diamond was born and raised in Cleveland, Ohio and desires a career that allows her to promote self-love as a modality for healing in urban areas.

Featured Student Authors

Destiny Brown (cover art illustrator)

Destiny Brown is a graduate of Cleveland Institute of Art and currently resides in Cleveland, Ohio. Her work can be seen on Instagram @ destiknee_b. Commissions can be requested by emailing destinysbrown95@gmail.com.

References

References

[i] Cone, J. H. (1999). *Risks of faith : the emergence of a Black theology of liberation, 1968-1998*. Boston, Mass. : Beacon Press, [1999].

[ii] Lorde, A. (2007). *Sister outsider : essays and speeches*. Berkeley : Crossing Press, [2007].

[iii] hooks, b. (2015). *Feminism is for everybody : passionate politics*. New York, NY : Routledge, 2015.

[iv] Cone, J. H. (1999). *Risks of faith : the emergence of a Black theology of liberation, 1968-1998*. Boston, Mass. : Beacon Press, [1999].

[v] Teo, T. (2011). Empirical race psychology and the hermeneutics of epistemological violence. Human Studies, 34(3), 237-255. Doi:10.1007/s10746-011-9179

References

[vi] Baszile, D. (2006). Rage in the interest of black self: curriculum theorizing as dangerous Knowledge. JCT: Journal of Curriculum Theorizing, 22(1), 89-98.

[vii] Somé, M. P. (1995). *Of water and the spirit : ritual, magic, and initiation in the life of an African shaman.* New York : Penguin, 1995.

[viii] Benson, R. I. (2015). *Fighting for our place in the sun : Malcolm X and the radicalization of the Black student movement, 1960-1973.* New York : Peter Lang, [2015].

[ix] Shahid, K. T. (2013). The power of revolutionary thought: Waging curriculum warfare on racial injustices in academia. In T. S. Poetter, T. S. Poetter (Eds.) , *Curriculum windows: What curriculum theorists of the 1960s can teach us about schools and society today* (pp. 1-15). Charlotte, NC, US: IAP Information Age Publishing.

References

[x] Walton, S. F. (1969). *The Black curriculum: developing a program in Afro-American studies.* East Palo Alto [Calif.] Black Liberation Publishers [c1969].

[xi] Ani, M. (1994). *Yurugu : an African-centered critique of European cultural thought and behavior.* Trenton, N.J. : Africa World Press, [1994].

[xii] Ani, M. (1994). *Yurugu : an African-centered critique of European cultural thought and behavior.* Trenton, N.J. : Africa World Press, [1994].

[xiii] Chabad.org article by Eliezer posner

[xiv] Somé, M. P. (1999). *The healing wisdom of Africa : finding life purpose through nature, ritual, and community.* New York : J.P. Tarcher/Putnam, 1999.

[xv] Langston Hughes. (2010). *Scholastic Scope, 59*(4), 17.

[xvi] Kelley, R. G. (2002). Freedom dreams : the Black radical imagination. Boston : Beacon Press, [2002].

References

[xvii] Sembène, O., Diop, M. T., Jelinck, A., Sene, M. N., Fontaine, R., Bissainthe, T., & ... Sembène, O. (2015). *Black girl ; Borom Sarret.* [London, England] : British Film Institute, [2015].

[xviii] Ani, M. (1994). Yurugu : an African-centered critique of European cultural thought and behavior. Trenton, N.J. : Africa World Press, [1994].

[xix] Adichie, C. N. (2015). *We should all be feminists.* New York : Anchor Books, [2015].

Shahid, K. (2014). *Finding Eden: How Black Women Use Spirituality to Navigate Academia.* (Electronic Thesis or Dissertation). Retrieved from https://etd.ohiolink.edu/

[xx] Lorde, A. (2007). The Master's Tools Will Never Dismantle the Master's House. *Sister Outsider: Essays & Speeches*, 110-113.

References

[xxi] Coogler, R., Cole, J. R., Feige, K., Boseman, C., Jordan, M. B., Nyong'o, L., & ... Carter, R. (2018). *Black Panther.* Burbank, CA : Marvel Studios, [2018].